Gerrie
Parker

Writing
Worthwhile
Behavioral
Objectives

Julie S. Vargas
West Virginia University

Writing
Worthwhile
Behavioral
Objectives

Harper & Row, Publishers
New York / Evanston / San Francisco / London

To
My Husband and My Father

Contents

This is a self-instructional book designed to help you write worthwhile, behaviorally stated teaching objectives that will increase the value of your courses and their relevance to your students' life outside school. Additionally, it teaches you to state these objectives in a way that increases the likelihood of their being achieved by your students.

It does not teach how to write objectives for *attitudes* (though the topic is considered briefly); it is restricted to what is often called the "cognitive domain."

The book itself is an example of the kind of individualized instruction that behavioral objectives make possible. It presents a sequence of objectives for you to reach—from identifying behaviorally stated objectives to writing a complete unit of behavioral objectives, which includes "understanding," "concept formation," and "creativity."

The book has its own objectives as well. More specifically, we might say that the general objective for Chapters 1–6 is teaching you to state objectives behaviorally. After completing these chapters you should be able to reach the behavioral objectives of:

1. selecting from a list of ten to twenty objectives the five that are the most behavioral
2. telling which of the necessary criteria (referring to the behavior of the student, describing observable behavior, and specifying a level or criterion of acceptable performance) a given objective meets or fails
3. revising nonbehavioral objectives
4. writing behavioral objectives for general objectives or test items.

The general objective for Chapters 7–9 is teaching you to identify what makes an objective worthwhile. After completing

these chapters you should be able to reach the behavioral objectives of:
1. classifying given objectives in the major categories of Bloom's taxonomy of educational objectives
2. replacing what Bloom calls "knowledge level objectives" with objectives that fall in the higher categories of Bloom's taxonomy
3. given a textbook chapter, writing objectives for a unit using that chapter.

The unit should have all levels of Bloom's taxonomy represented.

This book contains both text and exercises. The text presents the arguments for quality objectives; the exercises teach you how to write them. To avoid unnecessary practice, each chapter of exercises begins with a pretest covering the skills taught. If you score 90 percent or better on the pretest, skip the chapter and go on to the next. If you score less than 90 percent, then do the exercises. And, of course, you can work through the book at your own speed.

I would like to thank my students for consciously or unconsciously guiding the writing of this book. Their problems in writing objectives determined what topics and exercises were included, and their objectives provided many of the examples throughout the book.

Julie S. Vargas

Writing
Worthwhile
Behavioral
Objectives

How Objectives Help the Teacher

THE ROLE OF THE TEACHER

A teacher is one who expedites learning. If we accept current definitions, learning is (or involves, depending on your psychologist) a change in behavior. A teacher's job, then, is to change behavior. Some of the behavior a teacher wishes to change occurs in the classroom, but some occurs outside; and many important changes occur a long time after student and teacher have parted. Most of the behavior we desire outside the classroom is described by attitudinal words such as "showing an interest." To get a student to show interest in science, for example, means to change his behavior so that he engages in science-related activities not only inside but outside the school. We say he is interested in science if he joins science clubs, subscribes to science journals, takes more science courses, majors in science, or becomes a scientist. In changing attitudes, a teacher changes behavior.

Just as an artist or scientist is judged primarily by his products, so the measure of a teacher is his product—the change in his students' behavior. Most people would think it absurd to judge an artist by his method of mixing paints, his way of holding the brush, or his way of dressing while painting. Yet in education, teachers are judged by analogous techniques or characteristics. They are rated on use of audio-visuals, lecture style, neatness of displays or bulletin boards, and even on things as remotely related to student learning as their dress. Where, meanwhile, is the learning? Techniques used by the artist or teacher are important, but only insofar as they affect their products. The most effective teacher is the one who produces students who have learned most and who go on learning, regardless of whether he works with chalk and chalkboard or with the latest audio-visual techniques. Insofar as good audio-visual materials help change the behavior of the pupil, they are valuable, but evaluation should focus on the change, not on the factors related to it.

To change behavior effectively, a teacher must concentrate more on his students' behavior than on his own. He cannot rest content with the knowledge that he has "exposed" them to American history or fractions. "Exposure" is really a description of his own behavior, not that of his students. What were the students doing while they were being "exposed"? Perhaps they were sleeping, perhaps learning. To find out how much students have learned, the teacher must look at what they do.

HOW OBJECTIVES HELP THE TEACHER

In planning a course or class, a teacher has certain objectives he wishes to accomplish. These objectives may be printed in the school curriculum or textbooks or stated at the first meeting of the class; or they may just be general feelings the teacher has about what he wants his students to learn. In whatever form, objectives indicate what is desired at the end of training. They differ from "activities," which are the means of arriving at objectives. "Reading Shakespeare's *Macbeth*" is an activity; what the teacher wants the student to get out of reading the play is the objective.

Specific objectives perform three functions: They help the teacher select appropriate learning experiences, they communicate to others (particularly to the student) what is expected, and they give both student and teacher standards for evaluating progress.

Selecting Learning Experiences: Even when content, teaching materials, and class structure are set by the administration, the teacher has a good deal of freedom in selecting learning experiences. In the typical public school, he may choose whether his students learn primarily from lectures, movies, demonstrations, reading, discussions, exercises, or independent study. Even in courses with large enrollments, such as college lecture courses, the teacher can still vary assignments and course requirements.

When the teacher is clear about what he wants his students to do, he can more easily select relevant learning experiences than when goals are unspecified. With only a vague goal of "learning about opinion surveys," for example, a teacher might be content to "cover" surveys in a lecture or discussion group. if he then asks himself what his *students* should be able to do, he might discover that he wants them to be able to design and administer a simple opinion questionnaire. The lecture or discussion, which seemed appropriate before, now looks inadequate, and the teacher is likely to replace it by a more relevant experience, such as carrying out a simple survey.

When objectives are specified, time is used efficiently. When objectives are not clear, it is easy, particularly in small classes, to get sidetracked onto irrelevancies or to fall into ruts worn deep by tradition. When it comes time for evaluation, poor student performance on important skills may come as a big surprise. In one school midyear tests were required. Grades were set by the administration according to percent correct. One sixth-grade teacher was amazed when, upon correcting his tests, he found that twenty-seven of his twenty-nine students scored below 60 percent. He had to mark twenty-seven midyear tests "F." He had spent the term discussing the subject and going through the text, but until he wrote the midterm exam, he had not set up performance standards. If he had specified his objectives sooner, he would have emphasized more relevant activities, and most of his students would have passed.

Communicating to Others: Some teachers play the game of "guess what'll be on the test?" They give assignments and hold classes but give little indication of what is expected of their students. The students are to decide what is important. Leaving it to the student to decide what to learn is in direct contradiction to the teacher's job of helping him learn. To help a person learn something, let him know what he is expected to do. Most students want to please the teacher, if only to get a good grade. They will direct their effort toward what the teacher considers important—if they know what it is. If the teacher does not tell them, they may go to great efforts to find out. Because tests are usually the main standards of success, students will ask others about past tests. "He says he wants you to have some conception of the impact of the Civil War, but what he really wants is for you to remember the dates in the chart in the text." "Don't worry about *Othello,* he only tests on the plays he goes over in class." Statements such as these arise only when the teacher does not communicate his objectives. Part of helping students learn is guiding them in what to study, and guidance should come from the teacher.

Letting the student know what you expect of him is not "teaching for the test." A test samples only a few of the skills a student learns. The objectives should state the *kinds* of performances expected of the student. In meeting them, he should be able to solve not only the problems on a specific test, but any problems that use the same concepts and principles.

Clearly stated objectives improve communication not only to the student but also to parents, educators, and the general public. With the question "What am I getting for my tax dollar?" being asked more frequently, it soon may be critical for schools to be able to give the kind of unambiguous answers that specific objectives make possible.

Providing a Measure of Achievement: Objectives not only guide teacher and student in the teaching-learning process, but they also provide a measure against which progress can be judged. If the teacher is to improve his teaching, he must have information on the success of the different things he tries. Clear objectives help provide this information. They help make progress visible so that success can be seen immediately, not only at the end of the semester. Because seeing improvement encourages further effort, clear objectives motivate both teacher and student.

Accurate assessment of what each student can and cannot do is critical for good teaching. It is wasteful and it causes boredom or frustration to tell a student what he already knows or to talk over his head. Rarely can a teacher accurately "feel" where his students are. Many teachers have had to interrupt a class to backtrack to simpler steps or to ask if students already know the material. With objectives clearly in mind, much of the guesswork is eliminated. No matter what level the student has reached, the next step to be taken toward the desired final performance is clear.

WHAT KINDS OF OBJECTIVES BEST HELP THE TEACHER?

Imagine that you are a sixth-grade teacher teaching American history. Which of the following objectives would give you a clear idea of what learning experiences to select? Which would give the student an idea of just what to study? Which would give a clear criterion against which to measure student achievement?

A. To grasp the significance of George Washington's role as father of our country.

B. To outline four legal precedents established by George Washington while he was President.

Objective A is open to many interpretations. A teacher could concentrate on George Washington's military career, his Presidential decisions, or his contributions in the field of economics or law. Objective A narrows the subject to George Washington and American history, but it does not give much help in selecting learning experiences. What behavior shows "grasping the significance," and what constitutes being "father of our country"?

Objective B is one of many possible specific objectives which could be derived from Objective A. It states what the student is to learn to do, and it narrows down the content area. Once an objective is specified, the teacher can choose appropriate learning experiences. When he knows where he is going, he can concentrate on getting there.

Just as the person who writes Objective A fails to communicate well with the teacher, so he also fails to communicate with the student. Told to "grasp the significance of George Washington," the student must still find out what the teacher wants him to do. To help the student study effectively, an objective must not be ambiguous; it must indicate specifically what behavior is desired.

When it is clear what students should be able to do upon completion of a course, evaluating progress is no problem. For each specific objective the teacher asks, "Can he or can't he do this?" Think of writing a test item that would satisfy you that Objective B above had been reached. Now think of one for Objective A. For Objective B, all one has to do is drop the word "to," but writing a question satisfactorily covering Objective A is a problem.

Let us look at the problem another way. Which of the following test items is suitable for testing Objective A?

Test Items

A. George Washington became the first President of the United States in the year _____.

B. The effect of George Washington is still felt in our laws regarding
    a. segregation
    b. transportation
    c. separation of church and state
    d. election of a President.

C. Outline (in about two sentences each) four legal procedures set by George Washington while he was President.

If you find it difficult to decide, it is because any of the items could legitimately apply to Objective A. Because it is impossible to test unobservable internal states such as "grasping significance," the teacher still must decide what observable behaviors he desires. When he has specified what behaviors constitute "grasping significance," he has formulated his behavioral objectives.

A behavioral objective is a statement of what the student should be able to do at the end of a unit of teaching. It describes behavior. Moreover, it is observable behavior, such as outlining or calculating. It implies learning experiences, it can be communicated to the student, and it indicates a method of measurement. Hence, it satisfies our three criteria of a useful objective.

THE USE OF GENERAL OBJECTIVES

Few of the objectives found in most current curricula are behavioral. Most are so general that they provide little or no help to the teacher in his daily work, and as a result, they are often filed away unused.

The Derivation of Behavioral Objectives from General Objectives

Overall Objective: Understanding the Concept of Propaganda

General Objective: Being Aware of an Author's Bias		*General Objective: Recognizing Various Types of Propaganda*	
Behavioral Objective: Student should be able to circle the sentences in a paragraph of propaganda that reveal bias and tell which viewpoint the author holds.	Behavioral Objective: Student should be able to point out in a slanted article: 1. statements that are presented because of universal endorsement ("We want our children to be happy") 2. conclusions the author makes that do not necessarily follow (. . . so we should not allow them to work at jobs such as delivering papers) 3. hidden assumptions (paperboys are not happy).	Behavioral Objective: Student should be able to label sample advertisements or paragraphs as not propaganda or as one of the following types of propaganda: bad name glad name bandwagon testimonial plain folk card stacking	Behavioral Objective: Student should be able to mark words in a given article that show it as an example of: bad name propaganda glad name propaganda etc.

General objectives, such as Objective A, are nevertheless often useful in the initial design of a course. They give some idea of what the course is about, and they are easy to write. For teaching, however, more specific objectives need to be developed. One way to derive behavioral objectives is shown on page 9. For the overall objective of understanding the concept of propaganda you might proceed as follows to reach a behavioral restatement. First, ask yourself "What do I mean by 'understanding the concept of propaganda?'" Perhaps the answer is "being aware of an author's bias" or "recognizing various types of propaganda." These, then, are general objectives which focus on a narrower content area, and for any overall objective many can be written. The general objectives, however, still do not specify exactly what behaviors are wanted. What skills constitute "being aware of an author's bias"? One behavioral objective might be "to be able to circle the sentences in a paragraph of propaganda that reveal bias and tell which viewpoint the author holds." Other behavioral objectives are shown on page 9. These, together with all the other behavioral objectives the teacher writes, then become an operational definition of "understanding the concept of propaganda."[1]

Equipped with his behavioral objectives, the teacher knows exactly what he wants of his students. He can then concentrate on what, after all, is the most rewarding part of being a teacher —helping students learn.

---

[1] For a more detailed discussion of developing a unit, see Chapter 9.

2

Questions About Behavioral Objectives and Some Answers

New ideas always seem to generate a certain resistance, and the suggestion that teachers and curriculum developers write behavioral objectives is no exception. Here are some common questions about behavioral objectives, with comments.

ARE BEHAVIORAL OBJECTIVES PICAYUNE?

Behavioral objectives, one argument goes, are so specific that they become trivial. In contrast, a nonbehavioral objective such as "understanding chemistry" has a broader significance. It is a worthwhile goal to work toward, whereas an objective such as "to be able to write the abbreviations for the elements" misses what is important in the field.

The criticism can be answered on two points. First, specificity and triviality are not the same thing. For example, the objective "the student shall be able to extract the natural gases out of any of the following compounds: H_2O, etc." is quite specific, yet it is a worthwhile objective in its own right, and it certainly is not trivial.

Second, even if some or all behavioral objectives were trivial individually, the aggregate of objectives for a unit would not necessarily be trivial. From any one general goal, many sub-objectives are derived. Each nut and bolt in a piece of machinery is insignificant in itself, yet it fulfills a necessary function, and when combined with all the others makes the machine possible. Similarly, some behavioral objectives may look insignificant taken one by one, but each may be necessary for total mastery of a subject.

ARE BEHAVIORAL OBJECTIVES UNWIELDY?

If, from every single general objective, we derive many behavioral objectives, does this not mean a large and unmanageable mass of material? Will it not be necessary to spend at least one lesson teaching students how to find their way around in the catalog of behavioral objectives?

The objectives for two units from an individualized instruction course are reprinted below. These are two of about a hundred units, which together make up the entire sixty-five-page mathematics curriculum from kindergarten through seventh grade. This averages about eight two-unit pages for each year of work. A fourth grader, working fifty minutes a day, might complete a unit (by scoring 85 percent or better on the unit test) in two weeks. One-half page of objectives for two weeks' work is not cumbersome.

Sample Units Using Behavioral Objectives[1]
A. Unit on the "Meaning of Numbers" for Kindergarten or First Grade

   Note: The numbers used will be 0 to 10.

   1. Counts orally from one to ten.
   2. Tells what number comes before or after a given number, or in between two numbers.
   3. Selects the numeral for the number of objects in a pictured set.
   4. Counts orally up to ten objects by pointing to each object as it is counted.
   5. Writes the numerals from 1 to 10 in order.
   6. Writes any numeral named (from 1 to 10).
   7. Identifies a set with zero members. Writes 0 to indicate the number of a pictured empty set.

[1] These units are slightly modified versions of those formerly used in the mathematics program at the Oakleaf School, Baldwin Whitehall School District, which were developed in cooperation with the Learning Research and Development Center at the University of Pittsburgh.

B. Unit on Fractions at Third Grade Level

Note: Fractions used will be simple fractions to twelfths, written either in numerals (½) or in words (one-half), and the figures used will be unfamiliar irregular shapes as well as regular familiar forms.

1. Selects the fraction that shows what part of a figure is shaded.
2. Selects the figure that has a given fractional part shaded.
3. Shades a specified part of a figure. The figure may or may not be divided by lines to aid the student.
4. Shades or draws a ring around a given fraction of a set.
5. Adds and subtracts any two fractions with the same denominator, with, and then without, picture aids. Reduces the sums or differences to lowest terms.
6. Finds fractional parts of whole numbers (up to 25) that have whole number answers. (⅔ of 9 = _____.)

DOES STATING ALL YOUR OBJECTIVES TAKE THE SPONTANEITY AND CREATIVITY OUT OF TEACHING?

Some teachers insist that they should not be bound by specific assignments but should feel free to take up whatever happens to be of interest at the moment. Behavioral objectives, they say, tie a teacher down and keep him from exploring topics that arise from the situation or from student interests. If a student brings a frog to science class, for example, the teacher should be able to interrupt the scheduled topic to talk about frogs. If several class members are interested in snakes, the teacher should be able to change the focus of a unit on reptiles to snakes.

Many teachers feel that objectives should be set by the student because the student is more likely to be motivated if he can choose what to study. Part of the job of teaching, however, is selecting from a subject area what is most important for students to learn. Having students set objectives is shifting onto them one of the teacher's responsibilities. Who is in the better position to know what is important in a field — student or teacher?

To insist that the teacher bear the final responsibility does not mean that students should have no role in setting objectives. The teacher can take into account his students' backgrounds and interests, but he must be the final judge of suitability. Studying snakes may serve the biology teacher's objectives as well as the reptiles used in the text, but it would be hard to defend dropping a week's planned activities in a unit on the Civil War to study the relative merits of various guns, just because someone happens to bring an old gun to class.

A good objective states a skill that can be mastered in many different ways. The particular examples and exercises a teacher uses are vehicles to reach the objective, but the objective should not be tied to any one of them. The teacher who wants students to be able to diagram sentences will not care whether they work on sentences from an English text or on ones they write themselves. The students may choose the sentences they wish to use, so long as the objective is satisfied. By concentrating on objectives instead of on materials, the teacher can try new approaches, particularly if students are having difficulty with the text or are losing interest. Rather than hamper creativity, objectives stimulate the teacher to design new and more efficient learning experiences.

Objectives need not be immutable. New objectives can be added and old ones discarded or changed. In class, the teacher can set aside planned objectives and activities if an issue of interest arises. The "freedom," or "spontaneity," that comes from lack of planning is illusory, for it leaves the teacher few alternatives. If no productive lines of inquiry emerge, he is left unprepared and, feeling insecure, is likely to clutch at any familiar routine: giving a lecture or asking his students to "read the text and answer the questions" or doing whatever else he has done in the past. Where is the spontaneity in that?

In writing behavioral objectives, a teacher must constantly ask, "What do I want my students to be able to do?" In taking time to think through the answer, most teachers find themselves coming up with new ideas. In looking at goals in behavioral terms, the teacher is forced to go beyond the framework of textbook content. This, in turn, stimulates rather than hampers creativity.

DO BEHAVIORAL OBJECTIVES MAKE ALL STUDENTS ALIKE?

One aim of education is to help each student develop his own abilities and his own interests. Many teachers feel that to set objectives that are the same for each student is to interfere with their natural growth and to force each into the same mold.

We want our students all to be alike—in some ways. We would like them all to be able to read, for example, or to add. For any course, there are certain basic skills we wish every student to learn, and we do not help individual development by failing to teach them. By providing each student with the basic skills in a subject, we give him both a realistic picture of what the area is like and the background to pursue successfully any interests he may develop in the area.

Teaching basic skills does not, of course, guarantee individuality. Individuality lies in the *differences* among people. Not all differences qualify, however. We do not consider Joe's unique ignorance of history an expression of individuality. If, however, Joe knows more about motorcycles or butterflies than most boys his age, or if he expresses a unique but informed viewpoint on politics, we call it individuality. The differences we seek include specialized interest and knowledge beyond that held by others.

The degree to which individuality and originality are promoted in a class depends on what behaviors a teacher encourages or requires. A teacher can demand adherence to a single viewpoint or product, or he can ask for and reward uniqueness. How writing behavioral objectives will affect the amount of individual expression he allows or encourages in class is not obvious. In specifying objectives, what is demanded of the student becomes clear, and any regimentation becomes conspicuous. If the teacher does not approve of regimentation, he may discover ways to eliminate it in the process of specifying objectives. If, on the other hand, he wishes all to parrot a particular view, writing objectives may make him more successful in getting students to do so, and thus make his students more alike than when objectives were unspecified.

In either case, specifying objectives does not necessarily imply standardization. Flexibility can either be written into the objectives themselves—for example, by having the student select his own project or viewpoint (see Chapter 8)—or provided by sequencing the objectives. Instead of having the same "track," or sequence, of objectives for everyone, various paths, or "branches," can be designed. Some objectives may be required for everyone and some only for students with particular interests or abilities; or objectives can be arranged into equivalent paths, any one of which satisfies course requirements.

DOES WRITING OBJECTIVES TAKE TOO MUCH TIME?

Many teachers who are convinced of the utility of behavioral objectives say they would write them if only they had a little more time.

To decide on what you want your students to get out of your course does take time, but once you have set behavioral objectives, you save time in teaching. With objectives in hand, there is no time wasted in deciding what to do. And when it comes time to write tests, the job is essentially already done. Whether or not the time saved in teaching a course equals the extra time required to write objectives has not been determined. If a teacher teaches the same course more than once, however, we can be sure that there is a clear gain. Most teachers will want to revise their objectives each time they reteach a course, but that is easy once the main job has been done. (Incidentally, the ease with which objectives can be revised speaks well for flexibility of the system.) In any case, the increased effectiveness of behavioral objectives makes the time spent worthwhile.

3

Attitudes

The most important goal of education, according to many teachers, is the formation of positive attitudes. Most textbook writers cite the development of respect or appreciation for the subject as one of their basic aims. The concern for attitudes is a concern over the lasting effects of teaching. There is a difference between what students can do and what they will do once they have left school. It is not enough for a child to score at the twelfth-grade reading level in school if he hates to read when he leaves. A teacher feels he failed if a student gets an "A" in his science course but later scoffs at scientific methods and accomplishments. If the reason for schooling is to help each individual function effectively in his daily life and contribute to society, we must be concerned with what he will do when he is no longer in school. We must, in other words, be concerned with attitudes.

HOW WE DETERMINE ATTITUDES

In everyday language we talk about "having an attitude" as if it were a certificate to be carried around and exhibited from time to time. But an attitude is not a thing. It is a complex set of tendencies, which may or may not be under "voluntary" control, to act and react in certain ways. The person with a favorable attitude toward American literature has a high predisposition to read, to talk, or to think enthusiastically about it. The person who enjoys science is likely to talk about it, to read or listen to science news, to subscribe to science magazines, and so forth.

A tendency to act can exist even though at the moment an individual is not acting. We say an avid reader loves to read even when he is not reading. Similarly, a person's attitude toward science does not change when he stops working on a science project and takes a lunch break. The potential for science-related activities is part of the individual even when he is doing other things.

When a person does react to a given subject, we say he is "expressing an attitude." It is, of course, only through expression of attitudes that we know they exist. The only evidence we have for tendencies, even in ourselves, is past or present behavior.

Many different kinds of behaviors are involved in expressing attitudes. Some behaviors, such as "buying books," can be observed by others, but many important ones, such as "thinking about books," are private in that they can be "observed" only by the person who behaves. Statements such as "I think a lot about books and read a lot" or answers on attitude questionnaires are another class of behaviors indicating attitudes. They are not a measure of thoughts; they are talking and writing behaviors that may or may not correspond to thoughts or actions described. Some expressions of attitude are voluntary, such as praising a book. Some are involuntary, such as reflexes in anger or fear. A person who loves to read may react to news of the burning of a great library by an involuntary increase in heart beat, muscle tension, widening of the pupils of the eyes, and so forth. Attitudes may be expressed in an enormous number of behaviors.

In addition to the form of the behavior, the circumstances in which it occurs are a critical part of an expression of attitude. A behavior usually associated with favorable attitudes may occur in a circumstance in which it has a different meaning. The statement "I think a lot about books" may have one meaning when said in private to a friend, but a very different meaning when uttered just before semester's end to a reading teacher who grades on "attitudes." Only in the first case do we feel confident that the statement indicates a true attitude in the sense of indicating a strong tendency to read. In the second case, it is likely to mean "I would like to get a good grade and am trying to please you." The statement is the same, but the circumstances are different and the meaning we attribute to the behavior thus differs.

Just as a person may behave "as if" he had a favorable attitude, a person may be predisposed to act favorably, but not do so because of unfavorable circumstances. The lover of literature may be kept so busy (say, in army basic training) that he not only does not read but also does not even think much about it. To determine attitudes, then, we must look not only at what a person does but also at the circumstances under which he does it.

OBJECTIVES FOR ATTITUDES

It is not difficult to determine specific behaviors we normally consider evidence of goals such as "enjoy" or "take an interest in." We can imagine a person who "enjoys" or "takes an interest in" a topic such as classical music, and we can write down the behaviors that reflect this interest. Perhaps he talks about classical music a lot, states that he likes it, plays it, listens to it in preference to "pop" music, and so on. We may even be able to state which of these behaviors we would like to see in our music students as a result of taking our course on classical music. We can, in other words, specify behavioral objectives for attitudes. As soon as we *require* these behaviors, however, we alter circumstances, and their meaning changes. To take an extreme example, we often judge enjoyment by smiles and laughs. If, then, we state as a behavioral objective: "The student shall smile and/or laugh at least six times each class period" (and particularly if we grade on it), we are likely to end up with grimacing students forcing hollow laughter. Similarly, "optional" attending of concerts or reading of books outside class (a common index of motivation) is no longer optional if it is required for a passing grade. Even if we do not grade on attitudes, by specifying behavioral objectives for attitudes we encourage the student to engage in them to please us, not for the enjoyment he gets out of them. Hence, we cannot be sure of their meaning.

To be sure that the behaviors we use to indicate attitudes reflect "true" attitudes (the likelihood of similar behaviors *after* the student leaves the school), we can phrase them in the future or keep them to ourselves. The comment "I hope this course will stimulate you so that ten years from now you read at least one American writer each month" is less likely to create pressure to read for a grade than "I hope that while you take this course you will read at least one American writer each month, although I won't grade on it." Alternatively, we can write the latter objective without telling the student, and can inconspicuously keep track of the optional books students read. In neither case are attitude objectives used as a teaching tool in the same way as achievement objectives. They cannot be set up as objectives the student is to meet during the term.

ACHIEVEMENT OBJECTIVES AND ATTITUDES

Although we cannot set behavioral objectives for attitudes as part of the requirements for a course, we can still encourage positive attitudes by the kinds of achievement objectives we set and the way we conduct our classes. When we ask what it is that makes one student pursue a subject on his own and another avoid it whenever possible, we are looking for the causes of behavior. We want the student to engage in certain behaviors for their own sake—to "enjoy" what he is doing. Although a complete analysis of behavior is beyond the scope of this book, some of the effects on attitudes of setting behavioral objectives for achievement are discussed below.

BEHAVIORAL OBJECTIVES AS MINIMUM CRITERIA FOR A COURSE

In order to enjoy an activity, a student must do it. He will not do what he cannot do, and he will not be likely to do what he does badly or with great difficulty. In order to enjoy reading American literature for its own sake, a student must have a minimum skill level in reading. How many people *enjoy* reading a book (say, in a foreign language) when they have to look up the meaning of every tenth word? The poor reader is faced with a similar obstacle when reading a Hemingway novel. By insuring that our students at least *can* read at a high enough level of skill to understand Hemingway easily, we increase the likelihood that they *will* read him. Writing behavioral objectives forces us to specify skills necessary for proficiency in an area. To the extent that this encourages us to make sure that each student reaches them, behavioral objectives help insure those skills that make doing something possible.

It is not enough, however, to make sure that each student performs at a given level while in class. Within the school walls there are many reasons for reading. The student may read to get a grade, to avoid the embarrassment of not having read, to gain teacher or peer approval, and so on. If we want to tell how much he enjoys reading, we must look at what is controlling his behavior. Some of what is controlling his reading has nothing to do with reading itself; it is "artificial" or "extrinsic." Grades, avoiding the embarrassment of not having done homework, and teacher approval are all "added" consequences, which occur only in the school situation. If the student is reading because of them, he will not read when they are no longer present.

If we wish a student to continue to engage in an activity after he leaves school, either we must see that the student "enjoys" the activity for the natural consequences of doing it or we must make it useful outside school so that it is socially rewarded. By developing our students' skills in a nonpunitive way, we make the students predisposed to continue to engage in an activity. By making the activity relevant, we make it likely to be rewarded and maintained by society. Relevance, in turn, is determined by what we teach (see Chapter 7), not by the way we state objectives.

A student is not likely to enjoy an activity he was "forced" to learn or one associated with punishment or failure. Think of a subject you tend to avoid. It is probably a subject in which you were not very successful. One reason a student may not succeed is that objectives are not clear. The student may not be able to tell what the teacher wants or to see or feel progress. He may waste time and energy on things the teacher does not consider important and fail to perform in the areas in which the teacher grades. Frustrated, he is likely to feel resentment or hostility, some of which will be directed toward the subject itself. In contrast, when the behavior expected of the student is clearly stated, he is more likely to spend time efficiently and to see his progress. While he may still not work hard enough to be successful, he at least knows what needs to be done and thus avoids the frustration of ambiguity.

SUMMARY

Attitudes *are* important. If we are to produce adults who function effectively in society and who contribute to it, we must be concerned with what our students do after they leave us. In addition to teaching specific skills, we hope to create positive attitudes—that is, a high tendency to use those skills and to pursue an area further.

Outlining specific behaviors that usually indicate positive attitudes is valuable for measuring students' attitudes and interest in a course, but only if students are *not* under any pressure to produce the behaviors designated. Behavioral objectives for attitudes, in contrast to objectives for achievement, should not, therefore, be set as requirements for a course.

Although the way in which the teacher controls his students—whether through reinforcement or punishment—is probably the most important factor in creating attitudes, the kinds of objectives he sets are also important. In addition, to the extent that objectives communicate clearly, they can help the student master a subject. Competence, in turn, makes it possible for the student to get the natural rewards from working effectively in a field. He can enjoy activity for its own sake as well as for its usefulness in his life. Clear, worthwhile objectives, in other words, can help establish positive attitudes.

4

Identifying Behavioral Objectives

Pretest

Directions: Take this pretest and score it. (Answers are at the end.) If you score 90 percent or better (no more than two errors), skip to Chapter 5. If you miss three or more items, proceed with the exercises on the following pages.

Part I

Directions: From the following list of objectives, check the five that are most behavioral.

_____ 1. The student will jump over a high-jump bar three feet high.

_____ 2. The student will correctly thread the film on all movie projectors owned by the school.

_____ 3. The student will really understand the relationship between a meter and a yard.

_____ 4. The student will demonstrate that he thoroughly comprehends the concept of continent.

_____ 5. The student will tell the time to the nearest five minutes on a standard clock.

_____ 6. To know the significance of the Boston Tea Party for American history.

_____ 7. To write a paragraph of five sentences with no spelling or punctuation errors.

_____ 8. To gain insight into the Vietnam War.

_____ 9. To have a thorough evaluative grasp of Chaucer's role in the development of the English language.

_____10. To recite the poem "The Oak Tree."

Part II

Directions: Next to each objective below, write the letter of the improvement most needed to make the objective behavioral.

Improvement
A. Rewrite the objective to describe the activity of the student rather than that of the teacher.
B. Change unobservable goals to observable behaviors.
C. Specify the level or criterion of acceptable performance.

_____ 1. The student will know how to tie a shoe.
_____ 2. The student will perceive the fable of "sour grapes" as a lesson in psychology.
_____ 3. The student will be shown how to prove the Pythagorean theorem.
_____ 4. The student will understand how to milk a cow using electronic milkers.
_____ 5. To be able to read aloud.
_____ 6. To have a feeling for solving identities similar to those in Chapter V of the text.
_____ 7. To assist the student in naming the countries of Europe.
_____ 8. To evaluate critically, in writing, a poem similar to those in his reader.
_____ 9. To match the famous men of science with one-sentence descriptions of their contributions.
_____10. To have learned the names of the seven oceans of the world.

Answers
I. 1, 2, 5, 7, and 10. Score 1 point for each item correctly checked or left blank. Total = 10.
II. 1B, 2B, 3A, 4B, 5C, 6B, 7A, 8C (no standards for acceptable essays are given), 9C, 10B. Score 1 point each. Total = 10.

(Percent correct equals number of points times 5.)

Exercise 1
Comparing Objectives

Definition: A behavioral objective is a statement of what the student should be able to do upon completion of instruction.

Directions: Next to each pair of objectives below, write the letter of the objective that is stated more behaviorally.

―――― 1. a. The pupil will wash his hands before lunch.
         b. The teacher will emphasize the importance of good health.

―――― 2. a. The student will discover that objects of different weight fall at the same speed in a vacuum.
         b. The student will calculate the speed of objects of different weight falling in a vacuum.

―――― 3. a. The counselee will be more self-accepting and have a more positive self-image.
         b. The counselee will make no more than one negative comment about himself in half an hour of conversation.

―――― 4. a. The student will explain the relationship of the planets in the solar system.
         b. The student will be able to draw a diagram of the solar system with all planets labeled and in correct order in distance from the sun.

―――― 5. a. The student will recognize the formula for finding the volume of a cylinder.
         b. The student will select the formula for finding the volume of a cylinder.

―――― 6. a. The pupil will identify a selection of music as baroque, classical, romantic, or modern.
         b. The pupil will be assisted in developing an awareness of the period—Baroque, Classical, Romantic, or Modern—of a piece of music.

―――― 7. a. To improve the student's posture.
         b. To sit up straight during class.

_____ 8. a. To bring to class books from home.
    b. To acquire a taste for literature.
_____ 9. a. To keep on working when the teacher leaves the room.
    b. To help maintain an atmosphere of studiousness.
_____10. a. To explain the relationship of availability of goods to price of goods according to classical economics.
    b. To develop an understanding of the relationship of availability of goods to their price according to classical economics.

Answers: 1a, 2b, 3b, 4b, 5b, 6a, 7b, 8a, 9a, 10a

Exercise 2
Identifying Observable Behavior

To be behavioral, an objective must point to observable behavior on the part of the student—that is, an act that can be seen or heard.

Compare the following two lists:

Unobservable	*Observable*
know	list
understand	identify (from a number of choices)
have mastery of	state
discover	distinguish between
acquire skills in	contrast
grasp the significance of	solve

The words in the first list refer to states of the individual. These states are not directly observable, however, but must be inferred from observable evidence. The only directly observable evidence we have is the behavior of the student. As teachers we must decide what behaviors we shall accept as evidence of "understanding" or "mastery." These kinds of behaviors then define what we mean by "understanding" or "mastery." They are behavioral objectives; they tell us what a student who has "understanding" can do and what a student without "understanding" cannot do.

Directions: Next to each of the following write O if the behavior is directly observable and N if it is not directly observable.

_____ 1. To have learned about science.
_____ 2. To construct a triangle.
_____ 3. To give examples of metaphors.
_____ 4. To be knowledgeable about the American Revolution.
_____ 5. To check the verbs in a list of words.

_____ 6. To comprehend.
_____ 7. To define.
_____ 8. To achieve mastery.
_____ 9. To realize.
_____10. To separate into categories.

Answers: 1N, 2O, 3O, 4N, 5O, 6N, 7O, 8N, 9N, 10O

Exercise 3
Identifying Behavioral Objectives

Directions: From the following ten objectives (selected, incidentally, from actual curricula), check the five that are most behavioral.

_____ 1. To make pupils conscious of correct form and usage in speech and writing.

_____ 2. To be committed to reading as a lifetime experience and to understand Francis Bacon's observation that "Reading maketh a full man."

_____ 3. To state which statements are facts and which are opinions in a given article or story at the fourth-grade level.

_____ 4. To be familiar with the forms and conventions of the major literary genres: verse, drama, scientific drama, and so forth.

_____ 5. To believe that everyone's reading can be improved.

_____ 6. To select from written choices the main ideas in a short selection at the fifth-grade reading level.

_____ 7. To compare in written form the opinions of journalists in several newspapers and magazines on a particular subject.

_____ 8. To employ sound thinking habits in meeting daily problems.

_____ 9. To locate specific entries in the card catalog of the school library.

_____10. To enunciate and pronounce words correctly (no more than two mistakes a page) when reading orally in Book III of the reading series.

Answers: 3, 6, 7, 9, 10

To be behavioral, an objective must

A. refer to the behavior of the student rather than that of the teacher
B. describe observable behavior
C. specify a level or criterion of acceptable performance.

A. Check *each* of the following that violates criterion A.

      ——— 1. The teacher will explain the use of the color wheel in interior decorating.
      ——— 2. The student is to be shown the proper way to apply a triangular bandage for a head wound.

B. Check *each* of the following that violates criterion B.

      ——— 3. To discover the formula for area of a triangle.
      ——— 4. To fasten his seat belt before a car starts to move.

C. Check *each* of the following that violates criterion C.

      ——— 5. To write neatly.
      ——— 6. To select the best hand tool in the shop for any operation involved in building a wooden object as complex as a box with a hinge.

Answers
A. 1 and 2. "Be shown" is in the passive tense. It is the teacher who is applying the bandage.
B. 3
C. 5. How neat is "neatly"? What criteria are used?

Exercise 5
Meeting the Criteria for Behavioral Objectives

Directions: Next to each objective below, write the letter of the improvement most needed to make the objective behavioral.

Improvements

A. Rewrite the objective to describe student rather than teacher activity.

B. Change unobservable goals to observable behaviors.

C. Specify a level or criterion of acceptable performance.

_____ 1. The teacher will demonstrate how to tie a shoe.

_____ 2. The student will comprehend simple French sentences similar to those in Chapters 1 and 2 of *Everyday French.*

_____ 3. The student will be shown the Red Cross method of giving artificial respiration.

_____ 4. The student will orally name the colors.

_____ 5. The student will jump over a high-jump bar.

_____ 6. To become familiar with the song "My Country 'tis of Thee."

_____ 7. To assist the pupil to count to ten by ones.

_____ 8. To have memorized the names of the first ten Presidents of the United States.

_____ 9. To show the pupil how to locate a book in the library.

_____10. To write an essay comparing the economies of the North and South before the Civil War.

Answers

1. A
2. B
3. A. "The student will be shown" is grammatically in the passive voice. It describes what the teacher is doing. What is the student doing while he is being shown the method of artificial respiration?
4. C. Naming all the colors of oil paints available to an artist

would be a far different objective from naming the seven colors of the rainbow.

5. C. How high is the bar?
6. B
7. A
8. B
9. A
10. C. What constitutes an acceptable essay? With no criteria the following student answer would meet the objective:

The North and South had different economies. The South raised cotton but the North did not. The North's economy was different from the South's.

Posttest

Part I

Directions: From the following list of objectives, check the five that are most behavioral.

_____ 1. The student will demonstrate that he can effectively handle the American money system.

_____ 2. The student will gain an appreciation of the importance of Galileo in the development of modern science.

_____ 3. The student will be able to comprehend the relationship between centigrade and Fahrenheit temperature scales.

_____ 4. The student will name two examples each of solids, liquids, and gasses.

_____ 5. The student will orally read temperatures on a Fahrenheit thermometer to the nearest ten degrees.

_____ 6. To understand the meaning of "citizenship."

_____ 7. To construct a graph of the number of slices of bread eaten by the student each day for a week.

_____ 8. To measure and record to the nearest inch the length of various lines.

_____ 9. To gain insight into the nature of heat.

_____10. To run one hundred yards in sixty seconds.

Part II

Directions: Next to each objective below, write the letter of the improvement most needed to make the objective behavioral.

Improvement

A. Rewrite the objective to describe student rather than teacher activity.

B. Change unobservable goals to observable behaviors.

C. Specify a level or criterion of acceptable performance.

_____ 1. The teacher will demonstrate how to throw a javelin so that it lands point-in-ground at least twenty feet from the thrower.

_____ 2. The student will write a story about his summer.

_____ 3. The student will thoroughly comprehend the relationship between the volume, pressure, and temperature of a gas.

_____ 4. The student will be shown how to bake an angel food cake meeting standards of texture and "doneness" described in the text.

_____ 5. To write an essay comparing the French and American revolutions.

_____ 6. To solve word problems using algebra (on paper).

_____ 7. To help the student to identify the five insects in the sixth-grade science text.

_____ 8. To have confidence in one's ability to mix paint to match the colors in the color wheel on the bulletin board.

_____ 9. To understand the difference between "is" and "are."

_____10. To know the names of the twenty-four largest bones in the human body.

Answers
I. 4, 5, 7, 8, and 10. Total = 10.
II. 1a, 2c, 3b, 4a, 5c, 6c, 7a, 8b, 9b, and 10b. Total = 10.

(Percent correct equals number correct times 5.)

5

Making Objectives Behavioral

Pretest

Directions: Take this pretest and score it. (Directions for scoring begin on page 43.) If you score 90 percent or better, proceed to Chapter 6; otherwise, do the exercises in Chapter 5 for the parts you missed.

Directions: Rewrite each objective below to make it an acceptable behavioral objective. It should state observable behaviors expected of the student and some level or criterion for performance, and it should not contain extra words.

Sample

To have a thorough conceptual grasp of the concept of behavioral objective and the ability to spot behavioral objectives as opposed to nonbehavioral objectives.

To check the five behavioral objectives in a list of ten objectives.

---

1. The student will show that he has conceptual mastery of the operations of addition and subtraction, and that he understands the processes involved, by solving one-step word problems using addition and subtraction (with numbers up to 50 and second-grade reading level).

2. The student will spell correctly from dictation.

3. The course will cover the solving of quadratic equations like those in the text.

4. To have an appreciation of the difference between nouns and verbs.

5. To write an essay on the American Revolution.

Directions for Scoring: The left-hand column gives the directions for scoring each question and the exercises to do for each part you missed. Sample acceptable objectives are given in the right-hand column.

Score:

1. 1 point for including "solve one-step word problems using addition and subtraction (with numbers up to 50 and second-grade reading level)." (If you missed this, do Exercises 1–4.)

    1 point for omitting "conceptual mastery of the operations of addition and subtraction and that he understands the processes in-

Sample Acceptable Objectives:

The student will solve one-step word problems using addition and subtraction (with numbers up to 50 and second-grade reading level).

volved." (If you missed this, do Exercise 3.)

2. 1 point for including "spell correctly from dictation." (If you missed this, do Exercises 1–4.)

    1 point for specifying what words should be spelled or the level of difficulty of the words. (Any level, of course, makes an acceptable objective, not just the one used in the sample opposite.) (If you missed this, do Exercise 4.)

    The student will spell correctly from dictation all the words in the fourth-grade speller.

3. 1 point for changing "course" to "student." (If you missed this, do Exercise 1.)

    1 point for "solve quadratic equations like those in the text." (If you missed this, do Exercises 1–4.)

    The student will solve quadratic equations like those in the text.

4. 1 point for changing "have an appreciation of the difference" to an observable behavior such as "label," "circle," or "list." (If you missed this, do Exercise 2.)

    1 point for indicating some level of difficulty of nouns and verbs to be used. (If you missed this, do Exercise 4.)

    To label the nouns and verbs in a list of sixth-grade words.

5. 1 point for "to write an essay on the American Revolution." (If you missed this, do Exercises 1–4.)

    To write an essay on the American Revolution, including three of the causes mentioned in the text.

1 point for what must be included
for an acceptable essay. (Any specifications will do.) (If you missed
this, do Exercise 4.)

(Total = 10 points. 90 percent is 9 or more points.)

Exercise 1
Stating Objectives in Terms of the Student

Since it is change in the student's behavior that shows learning, objectives should focus on the student, not on what the teacher or the course will "cover." To make a statement behavioral, make sure that it indicates what the *student* will be able to do as a result of having been exposed to the course content and activities.

Directions: Make each objective below into a behavioral objective by replacing teacher behavior with student behavior.

1. The teacher will demonstrate how to focus a microscope on a slide so that cell structure can be seen.

2. The student will be shown how to play open C on a flute.

3. To provide experiences in naming the trees on the school grounds.

4. To develop pupils' awareness of the following different verse forms: sonnet, ode, and quatrain.

5. To lead the student to utilize the library for locating information to answer questions about American Presidents up to
   Lincoln.

Answers
1. The student will (be able to) focus a microscope on a slide
   so that cell structure can be seen.
2. The student will play open C on a flute.
3. To name the trees on the school grounds.
4. To name from examples the following different verse forms:
   sonnet, ode, and quatrain (or to exhibit some other behavior
   such as listing the forms, defining them, and so forth).
5. To locate information to answer questions about American
   Presidents up to Lincoln. ("To utilize the library for locating . . . Lincoln" is acceptable, but more wordy than necessary.)

Exercise 2
Making Objectives State Observable Behavior

An objective that describes only an internal state of the individual does not indicate how he shows when he has reached that state. In the objective "to know what an overhead projector is," for example, the internal state is "knowing." But what skills demonstrate "knowing"? To make the objective behavioral, the teacher must change the unobservable "know" to an observable behavior such as "pick out" or "define" that he feels is proof of "knowing." The objective then becomes "to pick out all overhead projectors in an audio-visual equipment room" or "to define overhead projector" or any of a number of specific skills that are evidence of "knowing what an overhead projector is."

Make each of the following objectives into a good behavioral objective by changing unobservable states to observable behaviors.

1. To know a synonym for tepid (such as cool, lukewarm).

2. To learn the date on which Columbus discovered America.

3. The learner will demonstrate a grasp of the principles of alphabetizing (using words from the fourth-grade reader, all of which begin with a different letter).

4. The student will demonstrate a knowledge of the difference between the following parts of a division problem: quotient, divisor, dividend, and remainder.

5. The student will learn at least two positions George Washington is noted for having held: (a) Commander-in-Chief of the Continental Army in the American Revolution; (b) first President of the United States; (c) signer of the Declaration of Independence.

6. To demonstrate a knowledge of the first verse of "Jingle Bells."

Answers
1. To write (or state, select, and so forth) a synonym for tepid (such as cool, lukewarm).
2. To write (or state, select from a number of dates, and so forth) the date on which Columbus discovered America.
3. The learner will number (or arrange, list, and so forth), in alphabetical order, words from the fourth-grade reader all of which begin with a different letter.
4. The student will write the quotient, divisor, dividend, and remainder in a sample problem next to the words that tell what they are (or any observable evidence of differentiating between the parts of a problem).

5. The student will list (or name, select from a list of positions, and so forth) two of the following positions George Washington was noted for holding: (a) Commander-in-Chief of the Continental Army in the American Revolution; (b) first President of the United States; (c) signer of the Declaration of Independence.

6. The student will sing (or write, recite, and so forth) the first verse of "Jingle Bells" (alone, or with piano accompaniment).

One useful feature of a behavioral objective is its directness. Unnecessary words obscure what the student is actually to do and give the impression that he has learned more than is actually the case. A simple, low-level skill such as "labeling stories from the fourth-grade reader as true or make-believe" passes as a lofty objective with the aid of the following words: "The student will develop the power of critical thinking and gain a thorough understanding of the concepts of reality and fiction by labeling stories from the fourth-grade reader as true or make believe."

The additional words do not make the objective more worthwhile. As the word "by" indicates, the children are still just labeling stories. The rest of the statement should be eliminated to make that clear.

Directions: Cross out the unnecessary words and, if necessary, change one word in each objective below so that only behavior is specified.

1. The student will demonstrate an understanding of the concept of a quadratic equation by labeling equations as quadratic or not quadratic.

2. The student will realize the importance of safety factors in driving an automobile and show that he appreciates potential dangers of not following safety procedures by buckling his seat belt before putting the car in motion.

3. The student will hop on one foot ten times in succession without falling in order to demonstrate the development of balance, gross motor coordination, and rhythmic or timing skills.

Directions: Rewrite the following three objectives so that they are stated in terms of the student's observable behavior only, eliminating unnecessary words.

4. To develop modest competence in applying the principles of scientific inquiry and experimentation by developing the ability to design an experiment to test whether a specified gas such as oxygen is necessary for combustion.

5. To be shown which of a number of abstract geometrical designs shows the best balance in order to develop the student's idea of balance as a concept.

6. Students will define the humanistics of discovery through the use of experience gained in problem solving, and through the efforts of discovery itself, using problems such as those in Chapter 6 of the text.

Answers

1. The student will label equations as quadratic or not quadratic.
2. The student will buckle his seat belt before putting the car in motion.
3. The student will hop on one foot ten times in succession without falling.
4. To design (outline or perform) an experiment to test whether a specified gas such as oxygen is necessary for combustion.
5. To check the abstract geometrical design that shows the best balance (from a number of designs).
6. Students will solve problems such as those in Chapter 6 of the text.

Exercise 4
Specifying the Level or Criteria for Acceptable Performance

A behavioral objective should specify not only behavior but also the level of the performance required. Without an indication of level of difficulty, it is impossible to tell whether a student has met an objective. Can a student spell? The answer depends on the words to be spelled. For the words used at, say, the tenth-grade reading level, the answer may very well be "Yes." For all words the answer is almost certainly "No."

The need for indicating a level of acceptable performance is most critical in objectives requiring original writing or construction, and it is there that it is most likely to be omitted. Two students may "be able to design and construct a wooden box," but the products may differ considerably in quality, and one may not even be acceptable to the shop teacher. "Yes, you built a box," he may say, "but look at the joints! There is an 8-inch crack in this corner, and this nail is protruding." Teachers do have standards; they just need to put them into words. This objective might have read: "To design and construct a wooden box meeting at least the criteria of workmanship for the course: (1) no visible cracks; (2) no part of nails or screws exposed except at hinges and locks."

To add criteria for acceptable performance, the teacher must decide what he wants to see in his students' products. It is a help to imagine a very good and a bad job. Those qualities that only the good products contain can then be written as criteria. If these criteria are listed elsewhere, the objective can refer to the source instead of listing them again. The shop objective might have read "to design and construct a box meeting the specifications on page 7 in the text."

When criteria are present, the objective serves as a contract and helps the teacher grade fairly by checking to see whether each requirement is met.

Directions: Add a level of performance or a criterion of acceptability to the objectives below. For this exercise, what level or criteria you use is not important so long as one is specified.

1. To name the parts of the body.

2. Given a behavioral and a nonbehavioral objective as samples, to write an essay comparing the two. (Note: What points would you look for in the essay?)

3. To design and construct a lamp out of wood using the lathe. (For this and the next two objectives, you may refer to a fictitious source if you lack the background to invent criteria.)

4. To write an essay comparing love for a particular person with love for humanity in general.

5. To make a poster with a perfect rendering of the elements of design.

Answers

The Completed Objective Should Include:	*Sample Acceptable Objectives:*
1. A list or reference to what parts of the body are to be named.	1. To name the following parts of the body: eyes, ears, nose, forehead, chin, neck, head, arms, hands, fingers, stomach, waist, legs, feet, and toes. Or To name the parts of the body indicated on the diagram in the tenth-grade biology text.
2. The features with respect to which the two objectives are to be compared. Some characteristics do not make an objective behavioral. For example, it would not be important in the essay to compare the length in words of the sample behavioral and nonbehavioral objectives.	2. To compare behavioral and non-behavioral objectives on the following points: a. Is the objective stated in terms of the student? b. Does it specify observable behavior? c. Does it indicate a level or criterion of acceptable performance?
3. Some criteria for workmanship must be included.	3. To design and construct, using the lathe, a lamp that meets the criteria for workmanship set for the course. Or To design and construct, using the lathe, a wooden lamp that meets requirements such as: a. Stability: It does not tip over when tipped 15° and released.

b. Mechanics: You must be able to turn it on and off with one hand.

c. Safety and finish: It has no protruding edges sharp enough to rip a Kleenex or catch a sweater dragged over it. No wires should be exposed or be free to move where they might wear.

d. Design: The design should utilize the characteristics of the type of wood used — for example, it should highlight the grain.

4. Points on which the two kinds of love are to be compared should be specified.

4. To write an essay comparing love for a particular person with love for humanity, covering the points discussed in the text.

Or

To write an essay comparing love for a particular person with love for humanity, covering the following characteristics:

a. Is it temporary or eternal?

b. Is it spiritual or sexual in nature?

c. Is it important for personal happiness?

d. Does it contribute to the health of society?

5. Criteria for good design must be included.

5. To make a poster that meets the criteria for design on page 27 of the text.

Or

To make a poster that:

a. Has no more than one main center of interest
b. uses shapes of at least three different sizes
c. divides the total area into three unequal areas not arranged in order of size
d. uses at least two spacial planes.

Directions: For each objective below, first write the letter of each requirement it does not meet and then rewrite the objective to make it behavioral.

Requirements for Behavorial Objectives
A. They refer to the student's behavior.
B. They specify observable behaviors.
C. They state a level or criterion of acceptable performance.
D. They do not contain unnecessary words.

_____1. To define the apprenticeship method of learning a trade.

_____2. To explore the American style of writing through the expressive reading of poems such as those in Unit I.

_____3. To demonstrate to the student how to correct for parallax when less than 6 feet from a subject so that the subject photographed is centered from top to bottom within a quarter of an inch in a 3 x 5 picture.

_____4. To lead the pupil to an understanding of the steam engine.

Answers

1. C. Your objective should specify what constitutes an acceptable definition either by giving the definition, as in "to define 'the apprenticeship method of learning a trade' as 'the method in which a youth learns a trade by working as a helper to a master craftsman'," or by referring to a source, as in "to define the apprenticeship method including all the characteristics mentioned in the definition in the textbook."

2. C, D. The words "to explore the American style of writing" are unnecessary. Exploring is not what the student is doing. The objective also needs some qualifications for "expressive" reading. One possibility might be: "To read poems such as those in Unit 1, pausing only at commas or periods, and not pausing at the end of lines unless a phrase ends there."

3. A. "To take a picture at less than 6 feet in which the subject is not more than $\frac{1}{4}$ inch off center, top to bottom, in a three-by-five print" (or equivalent).

4. A, B, C. A sample answer correcting all three faults is "to label the twelve main parts of a steam engine listed on page 30 of the text on a scale or drawing or diagram similar to, but not identical to, those in the text."

Directions: Rewrite each objective below to make it an acceptable behavioral objective. It should state observable behaviors expected of the student and some level or criterion for performance, and it should not contain extra words.

Sample

To have a thorough conceptual grasp of the concept of behavioral objective and the ability to spot behavioral objectives as opposed to nonbehavioral objectives.

To check the five behavioral objectives in a list of ten objectives.

---

1. The teacher will demonstrate the division of two-digit numbers by one-digit numbers involving no remainder.

2. The student will show that he has grasped the concept of control in scientific discovery and has developed the ability to think scientifically by checking the procedure (out of three possibilities) that best answers a specific question.

3. To appreciate John F. Kennedy's accomplishments in the development of our country.

4. To parallel park a car within a standard 25-foot space on a city street.

5. To realize the distinction between "make-believe" stories and true stories.

Directions for Scoring

Score:

1. 2 points for changing from teacher to student behavior.

2. 1 point for omitting "show that he has grasped . . . through . . . think scientifically by."

   1 point for "check the procedure (out of three possibilities) that would best answer a specific question."

3. 1 point for changing "appreciate" to an observable behavior and 1 point for indicating which of Kennedy's accomplishments should be considered.

4. 2 points for adding at least two

Sample Acceptable Objectives:

The student will be able to divide two-digit numbers by one-digit numbers involving no remainder.

The student will check the procedure (out of three possibilities) that would best answer a specific question.

To outline at least three pieces of legislation introduced by John F. Kennedy while he was President, indicating what groups of people they would affect in economics, education, and civil rights.

To parallel park a car within a standard

criteria for an acceptable parking job.

25-foot space on a city street as follows:

a. Car should be backed in, with driver checking rear view mirror first.
b. Neither surrounding car should be touched hard enough to visibly move or jar it.
c. The car should be at least 1 foot from each surrounding car and with its wheels no more than 2 feet from the curb.
d. The car should not go up onto the curb at any time.

5. 1 point for making the behavior observable (such as "point to," "describe," "name").

1 point for indicating the level of reading difficulty.

To tell whether short stories such as those in the second-grade reader are true stories or "make believe."

6

Writing Behavioral Objectives

Pretest

Directions: Take this pretest and score it. (Directions for scoring are on page 70.) If you score 90 percent or better, proceed to Chapter 7; otherwise, do the exercises in Chapter 6 for the parts you missed.

Part I

Directions: Write an A in front of the five statements below that are more likely to be activities than objectives.

_____1. To write six reports in newspaper reporting style.

_____2. The student will give Dante's *Inferno* a thorough reading.

_____3. From several experimental designs, to select the one that will provide a control for a given variable.

_____4. To write the last line in an incomplete limerick with correct rhyme and scan.

_____5. To go on a field trip to the Museum of Natural History.

_____6. To do experiment 4: Let sealed cans of solids and liquids roll down a track and record which rolls faster.

_____7. To participate in a discussion on how to multiply negative numbers.

Part II

Directions: Under each Item below, write the behavioral objective for the skill tested. Include the level of difficulty of content to be used.

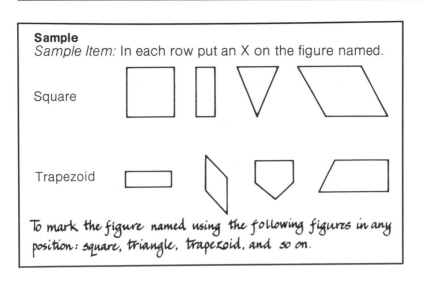

Sample
Sample Item: In each row put an X on the figure named.

Square

Trapezoid

To mark the figure named using the following figures in any position: square, triangle, trapezoid, and so on.

Item 1: Correct the spelling of the possessives in the sentences below by adding apostrophes where necessary.

a. The boys and mens bath houses in Marylands state parks are near the childrens bathing areas.
b. Mrs. Smiths sister is visiting the Thomas farm.

Objective for Item 1.

Item 2

WINTER by Lisa Justine

Winter is gray or so they say.
But have you looked out on a snowy day?
The snow is white, the sky is blue,
And last years' leaves are peeping through.
With a touch of brown and a tint of red
They're telling us that all's not dead.
The sunrise tones mixed in with grays
Foretell the colors of summer days.

List all the color words in the above poem.

Objective for Item 2.

Item 3: Write the missing letter in each word below as the word is read to you. (Teacher reads "cat, cot, sit, sat, set.")

1. c__t 2. c__t 3. s__t 4. s__t 5. s__t

Objective for Item 3.

Item 4: What would you have to do to prove whether or not atoms and molecules really exist?

Objective for Item 4.

Part III

Directions: Write one behavioral objective that could be derived from each general aim or activity below.

1. In this unit the student will read about the concept of civilization.

2. This lesson attempts to describe some of the implications of Newton's first law: A body at rest or in uniform motion will remain at rest or in uniform motion unless acted upon by some external force.

3. This book helps the child become aware that words must be arranged in a certain order to convey meaning.

Part I: *Directions for Scoring*
Items 1, 2, 5, 6, and 7 should have A's. Score 1 for each item correctly checked or left blank. Total = 7. (If you missed any of these, see Exercise 1.)

Part II: *Directions for Scoring*

Score (Total = 12):

Sample Acceptable Objectives:

1. 1 point for specifying that the student should be able to add apostrophes.

   1 point for indicating that the words will be in sentences.

   1 point for indicating either the kinds of possessives used or the general level of difficulty of the sentences. (If you missed this, see Exercise 3.)

   To add apostrophes to words in sentences (such as those in Chapter 2) to show correct possessives (all singular and double possessives will be used).

2. 1 point for "to list (write, circle, or otherwise identify) color words."

   1 point for indicating that the words will be in context.

   1 point for indicating some level of difficulty. For this point the objective should *not* restrict the skill to this poem. The objective "to list the color words in 'Winter' by Lisa Justine" gets only 2 points in all. (If you missed this, see Exercise 2.)

   To list all the color words in poems (or prose) at the third- (or fourth-, and so forth) grade level.

   Or

   To list all the color words in poems such as "Winter" by Lisa Justine.

3. 1 point for stating that the student must fill in missing letters from dictation.

   1 point for specifying that the letter written is to be a vowel.

   1 point for indicating the difficulty level of words used or that beginning and ending letters will be the same. (If you missed this, see Exercise 3.)

To write the missing vowel in three-letter words (consonant-vowel-consonant) as the teacher reads them, using words with the same beginning and ending letters (i.e., hit, hat).

4. 2 points for specifying that the student will be writing about a method for proving the existence of some particles.

   1 point for including some criteria for evaluating students' essays. (If you missed this, see Exercise 3.)

To outline a procedure for determining whether or not some hypothesized particles (such as atoms or molecules) really exist. The essay must include:
a. what to do
b. possible results and what they would mean.

Part III: *Directions for Scoring*

Score (Total = 6):

1. 1 point for indicating what the student will be able to do as a result of having read about civilization.

   1 point for specifying some criteria.

Sample Acceptable Objectives:

The student will be able to tell which of two peoples had the more highly developed civilization and defend his choice using the following as criteria:
a. degree of technological advancement
b. development of social roles
c. development of art forms.

2. 2 points for indicating what the student will do with Newton's law

To predict the line of motion of various objects under various hypothetical

(state implications, predict, give examples of it, and so forth).

conditions according to Newton's first law (for example, if you threw a ball in space, away from fields of gravity, what would happen to it?).

3. 2 points for what the child will do to show that the order of words is important for meaning.

To arrange three to five words (fourth-grade level or below) in two different ways: one to make sense and one to make nonsense.

(Total = 25 points. 23 or more points is above 90 percent)

Behavioral objectives specify student behavior, but they are different from activities. The difference is between ends and means. Objectives state skills you want your students to have, and activities are the means by which they are reached.

"The student shall read a biography of Lincoln" describes student behavior, but it is an activity because it does not indicate what the student will get out of his reading. What will the student be able to do as a result of having read the biography? That is the objective.

Directions: Next to each of the items below, write A if it is likely to be an activity or O if it is an objective or end in itself.

_____ 1. The student will practice his new spelling words three times each week.

_____ 2. The student will correctly spell the words in the list of new spelling words.

_____ 3. To run the mile in eight minutes or less.

_____ 4. To run around the track four times every gym period.

_____ 5. The student should be able to view the film "Molecules and Atoms."

_____ 6. The student should be able to write at least ten original behavioral objectives for a given instructional unit.

_____ 7. Each student will make four cups on the potter's wheel using the method outlined in Unit 5.

_____ 8. The student will do the exercises on page 60 of his workbook.

_____ 9. To take a school trip to an auto assembly plant.

_____10. To say the English equivalent of basic French vocabulary words (those listed in the textbook *First Year French*).

Some activities are designed primarily for "fun" or to change attitudes. For these activities it may be difficult, if not impossible to write a behavioral objective, but, if students like them, they are valuable nevertheless. If students do *not* enjoy an activity, or if they do not report that it made an impression on them, the activity is not worthwhile as entertainment and it is unlikely to be changing attitudes. Then, unless a behavioral objective can be stated for the activity, it is "busy work"—work without a purpose.

Answers

1. A. The spelling objective is to spell the words correctly. Practicing is a means of reaching that goal.
2. O.
3. O.
4. A. The objective or purpose for running is probably physical fitness, and could better be written as in number 3. (One might have an objective to get out and run at least four times a week, but that is an objective in self-discipline, not in running. It may, nevertheless, be a good objective.)
5. A. If this were an objective, all the student would have to do to meet it would be to keep his eyes open during the film.
6. O. Writing objectives, however, can also be an activity to teach the objective of being able to write objectives for a unit.
7. A. Requiring each student to make four cups shows that this is an activity. Some students may take four cups to learn the required level of skill in turning on the potter's wheel, some may take more, some less.
8. A. What will he learn by doing them?
9. A. One objective for the trip might be "to describe how an assembly plant increases productivity by the arrangement of materials and operations."
10. O. Being able to translate basic vocabulary words into one's own tongue is an end in its own right.

In most school districts, textbooks are selected for the teacher, and he must design his courses with them in mind. The objectives he sets, however, should outline skills that are not tied to a particular text or exercise. "To list all the color words in the poem 'Winter' by Lisa Justine," for example, is a poor objective. The teacher is not really interested in the words "gray," "red," "sunrise," and "rainbow" or that the student should remember them later. The relevant skill is not to list the words in *that* poem but the ability to identify "color words" in any poem. To give an idea of the level of difficulty of poems used, the objective can refer to a specific poem, but only as an example. The above objective could be rewritten, "to list the color words in poems *such as* 'Winter' by Lisa Justine."

Directions: Rewrite the following objectives so that they state skills that are free of specific instructional materials, problems, or examples.

1. The student should be able to solve the five word problems in addition and subtraction at the end of Chapter 3.

2. The student will be able to construct the stool pictured on page 10 of the shop textbook so that it meets the criteria for workmanship for the course.

3. To name three children who were at Sam's birthday party in the story "Surprise for Sam."

Sometimes we would like the student to remember a particular story, fact, or procedure. We might, for example, want our students to be able to name three characters in Shakespeare's *Hamlet.* The particular work *is* of concern. In contrast, the story "Surprise for Sam" in objective 3 above is used to teach comprehension skills, but is not worth remembering in itself.

Directions: Check each item below in which the particular instructional material is an *important* part of the objective.

_____ 4. To analyze the musical form of "Little Red Wagon Painted Blue."
_____ 5. To compare Dickens' view of English society with that of Trollope.
_____ 6. To state the message of *Uncle Tom's Cabin* and tell how it was used as propaganda.

Directions: Under each item below write the behavioral objective for the skill tested. Make sure the *particular* content is included only where it is important.

Item for number 7: Next to each word write the number of syllables it has.
_____silly   _____red   _____above   _____bicycle

7.

> *Item for number 8:* Next to each war below write the letters of the countries that sent troops into combat in that war.
>
> World War I _____   a. France
> World War II _____   b. England
>   c. Germany
>   d. U.S.A.
>   e. Russia
>   f. etc.

8.

Sample Answers
1. The student should be able to solve word problems in addition and subtraction similar to those at the end of Chapter 3 (or equivalent).
2. The student will be able to construct simple wooden articles such as the stool on page 10 of the shop textbook so that they meet the criteria for workmanship for the course.
3. To answer factual questions on stories such as the ones in the reader (or any other objective on comprehension but not on "Surprise for Sam").
4. No check. The skill is analyzing forms. Knowing "Little Red Wagon" is not important. Any other simple song could be used instead.
5. Item 5 could be checked if you felt that the students should remember Dickens' and Trollope's views, or not checked if you felt the crucial part of the objective was being able to compare two authors—any two authors.

6. Should be checked. The particular work is important here. Others could not be substituted.

7. The objective should include writing the number of syllables and the level of difficulty (up to three-syllable words at such and such a grade level), but should not be tied to the particular four words in the item. "To write the number of syllables in words *such as* 'silly,' 'red,' 'above,' or 'bicycle'" is acceptable, but "to tell the number of syllables in 'silly,' 'red,' 'above,' and 'bicycle'" is not.

8. These particular wars are probably important. If so, they should be part of the objective as in the following: "To select from a list of countries those that were involved in World Wars I and II." Another possibility is to view these two wars as only some of the wars the students should know about. Then the following would be more appropriate. "To match major wars (as defined in class) with the countries that sent troops to fight in them."

One way of developing behavioral objectives is to work from tests or exercises to see what kinds of behavior are required of the student. Any item from a test or exercise, however, is usually only one of a number of items that could be used to determine whether the skill is mastered, and it is the skill that the objective must capture. The particulars of the item, while not part of the objective, are important in that they indicate the level of skill required.

Item A

	12	13	23	73
Add:	14	11	10	16

In Item A above, for example, it is not important that the specific numbers be 12 and 14, 13 and 11, and so on, but it is important that they be two-digit numbers and that no "carrying" is involved. The objective for the skill that Item A tests might be stated "to add any two two-digit numbers without carrying."

Directions: Check the best behavioral objective for each Item below.

Item 1
Add: $2 + 3 =$ _____ $6 + 1 =$ _____
         $4 + 7 =$ _____ $5 + 5 =$ _____

---

1. Objectives for Item 1:
    _____a. To add two numbers.
    _____b. To add two one-digit numbers.
    _____c. To add 2 and 3, 4 and 7, 6 and 1, 5 and 5.

Item 2
If you wanted to know the name of the present secretary of state, in what reference would you look?

---

2. Objective for Item 2:
    _____a. To check which one of a given list of sources would contain the name of the present secretary of state.
    _____b. To name the reference in which the name of the present secretary of state would be found.
    _____c. Given a specific piece of information desired (such as the name of the present secretary of state), to name the reference in which the information could be found.

Just as there is a difference in the skill required to add with and without "carrying," so there is a difference between producing an answer and selecting one of a number of possible choices. Which item below would be easier for you to answer?

Item B: Write an original behavioral objective that meets the three criteria specified in this book.

Item C: Which objective below meets the three criteria for a behavioral objective as specified in this book?

1. To spell.
2. To spell any phonetic three-letter words that consist of consonant-vowel-consonant.
3. To perceive and hear the consonant and vowel sounds in three-letter, consonant-vowel-consonant words.

Identification items (Item C) are simpler than recall or original production (Item B), and an objective should indicate which is required.

Directions: Check the best objective for each Item below.

Item 3
Write the letter of the name of each part of the flower on the diagram.

a. Stamine

b. Pistil

c. Sepal

d. Petal

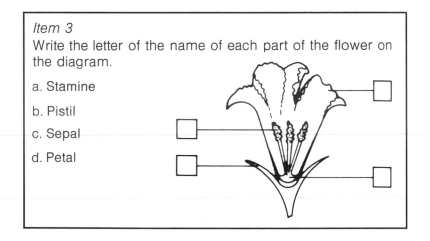

3. Objective for Item 3:
   _____a. To label the four main parts of a flower on a diagram.
   _____b. To match the four major parts of a flower with their names.
   _____c. To draw a diagram of a flower and label its four main parts.

Item 4
Write *your own* example of onomatopoeia (words used in class or in the text are not acceptable).

---

4. Objective for Item 4:
   _____a. To tell whether or not a given word is an example of onomatopoeia.
   _____b. To write the word for "the formation of a word to sound like some characteristic of the thing to which it refers (for example, cuckoo)."
   _____c. To write an original example of onomatopoeia.

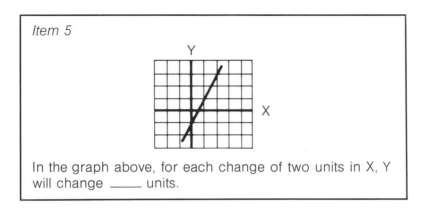

Item 5

In the graph above, for each change of two units in X, Y will change _____ units.

5. Objective for Item 5:
   _____a. From a graph of a first-order equation, to tell how many units one variable will change for given changes in the other.
   _____b. To tell how many units Y will change when X changes two units, given a graph of $Y = 2X - 1$.
   _____c. To select the number of units one variable will change for given changes in the other variable, given a graph of the relationship between the two (using first-order equations).

Answers
1. b
2. c. The skill is utilizing resources and is not concerned with the Secretary of State, but with where certain kinds of information are to be found.
3. b
4. c
5. a

Exercise 4
Writing Objectives from Test Items

Directions: Under each Item below, write the objective for the skill the Item is testing.

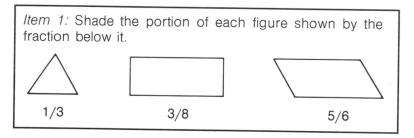

Item 1: Shade the portion of each figure shown by the fraction below it.

1/3   3/8   5/6

Objective for Item 1.

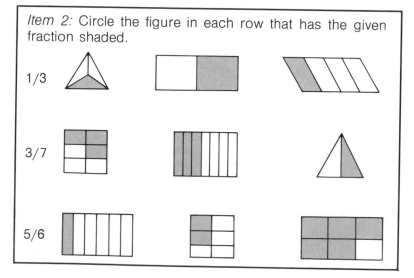

Item 2: Circle the figure in each row that has the given fraction shaded.

1/3

3/7

5/6

Objective for Item 2.

Item 3: Diagram the following sentences:
The dog ran.
Jane sang.
The apple fell.

Objective for Item 3.

Answers

Comments:

1. a. The objective should mention the kind of figures and fractions to be used.

   b. The objective should require shading figures. Since it is easier to shade divided figures such as the one below than un-marked ones, it might be worth-while to mention that the figures will not be marked in divisions.

Divided Figure

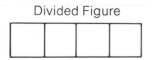

Sample Acceptable Objectives:

To shade given proper fractions (up to eighths) of regular figures which do not have divisions marked.

2. a. Here the objective is one of identification.

   b. Like the objective for Item 1, this one should specify the kind of figures and fractions to be used.

   To circle the figure that has a given fraction shaded (using proper fractions up to eighths and regular figures with divisions marked).

3. a. The degree of complexity of sentences to be diagrammed should be specified.

   To diagram sentences of up to three words (or simple sentences without clauses).

Part I

Directions: Write an A in front of the five statements below that are more likely to be activities than objectives.

_____ 1. The student will go through the flashcards on multiplication three times each week.

_____ 2. The student will spell the words on the sixth-grade spelling list.

_____ 3. To read two essays on the Spanish Inquisition.

_____ 4. To visit the local dairy and see the way cows are milked by machine and the way they are milked by hand.

_____ 5. To mark the subject and predicate in simple sentences such as those in the workbook.

_____ 6. To do the exercises at the end of each chapter in the text.

_____ 7. To watch the film "Molecules and Atoms."

Part II

Directions: Under each Item below, write the behavioral objective for the skill tested. Include the level of difficulty of content to be used.

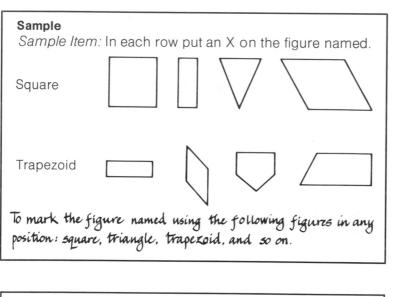

Sample
Sample Item: In each row put an X on the figure named.

Square

Trapezoid

To mark the figure named using the following figures in any position: square, triangle, trapezoid, and so on.

Item 1: Put the following words in alphabetical order by numbering them from 1 to 5:

_____cat
_____acorn
_____kite
_____wise
_____baby

Objective for Item 1.

Item 2: In each row, circle the word or words that have the same meaning as the first word.

effete	strong	hard	worn out	shut in
spurious	rapid	impure	not genuine	not allowed
indisposed	sick	valuable	not discarded	thrown out

Objective for Item 2.

Item 3

JOSEPH by Lisa Justine

Joseph was a little boy. He lived in a house with his mother and father. Joseph had one turtle and two goldfish. But Joseph was sad. Joseph didn't have a friend.

One day Joseph woke up very early. His mother was asleep. His father was asleep. But someone was awake. Joseph heard a man singing outside. Then he heard him call "good morning" to Chips their dog. It was the milkman. Joseph jumped out of bed and . . . (the rest of the story follows).

How did the milkman feel while he was working?
sad   happy   sick

Objective for Item 3.

> *Item 4:* Describe the system of "triangle trade" in the American colonies during the early seventeenth century, giving an original example to illustrate how it worked.

Objective for Item 4.

Part III

Directions: Write one behavioral objective that can be derived from each general aim or activity below.

1. In Section Four, the concept of percentage is developed.

2. The student will read several biographies of famous scientists.

3. This unit helps children take responsibility for participating in conversation and discussion, and to respect the ideas that others have to offer.

Part I: *Directions for Scoring*
Item 1, 3, 4, 6, and 7 should have A's. Score 1 point for each item correctly marked or left blank. (Total = 7.)

Part II: *Directions for Scoring*

Score (Total = 12):

1. 1 point for "to number (or arrange) in alphabetical order. . . ."

   1 point for indicating that the words all begin with different letters. It is much more difficult to alphabetize, for example, Macintosh, Mack truck, and McIntyre.

   1 point for indicating either the general reading level of the words or the number of words to be alphabetized.

2. 1 point for "to circle (or otherwise mark) the words that have the same meaning" (synonyms).

   1 point for indicating a difficulty level of the words used.

   1 point for indicating *either* that the choice will be between four words, or that the meaning will be in simple vocabulary.

Sample Acceptable Objectives:

To number in alphabetical order up to ten words at the fifth-grade reading level, all of which begin with different letters.

To circle from four choices the common meaning of given words at the twelfth-grade reading level. (Meanings will be at sixth-grade vocabulary level.)

3. 1 point for indicating that the student will be selecting answers to questions on a story.

   1 point for indicating a level of difficulty (reading level) of the story.

   1 point for *not* tying the objective to the particular story "Joseph." (It is also desirable to indicate that the answers to the questions will not be directly stated in the story, but that is a fine point.)

   To select the best answer to questions requiring inference from a story at the second-grade level.

   Or

   To select the best answers to questions on a story such as "Joseph" by Lisa Justine. The answers will not be directly stated in the story.

4. 1 point for "to describe the system of 'triangle trade.'"

   1 point for "give an original example to illustrate how it worked."

   1 point for indicating some point that must be included for an acceptable answer.

   To describe the system of "triangle trade" in the American colonies during the early seventeenth century, giving an original example to illustrate how it worked, including:
   a. countries participating
   b. products they produced for export
   c. products they did not produce enough of to meet their demands.

Part III: *Directions for Scoring*

1. 1 point for indicating what the student will be doing (calculating, defining, converting, and so forth).

   1 point for indicating a level of difficulty.

   The student will be able to calculate what percentage one amount is of another amount (using whole numbers only).

2. 2 points for stating something the student will be able to do as a result of having read the biographies.

To outline at least two similarities and two differences in the working habits of two of the scientists studied in the course.

3. 2 points for specifying some measurable action that you feel shows "taking responsibility for participating in conversation and discussion" or "respecting ideas that others have to offer."

To talk up at least three times in a ten-minute discussion without interrupting anyone.

What Makes an Objective Worthwhile and Relevant?

Two aspects of an objective determine its value for education: clarity and importance. By stating objectives behaviorally, we achieve the clarity necessary for selecting learning experiences, communicating effectively to the student, and evaluating student performance. Stating an objective behaviorally, however, does not guarantee that the objective is important. To take an extreme example, the objective "to write from memory all the entry words on page 6 of *Merriam Webster's Elementary School Dictionary* is behavioral, but few would argue that it is worthwhile. Such a skill has no use outside or even inside the school. To be worthwhile, an objective must contribute to the overall goal of education; it must help the individual function effectively in his daily life.

A hundred years ago it was relatively easy to determine the content of the education needed by a productive member of society. A teacher could predict a child's occupation from his father's occupation or social class. Because most occupations drew upon a relatively stable body of knowledge, the teacher knew what skills a student would need for the occupation he was to enter. Getting an education could consist largely of acquiring certain basic skills and memorizing solutions to standard problems the student would be likely to encounter. Today, it is nearly impossible to predict the future professions of our elementary or secondary school students. Although we can identify some general skills, such as reading and adding, that are helpful in any profession, we cannot tell what specialized content a student will need even if we can predict his future occupation. Occupations are changing rapidly, and information that is necessary today may very well not be used at all by the time the student begins a job.

When writers describe what children should learn in our schools today, they stress general goals such as understanding and creativity. No one would argue against these goals, but if they are to be useful, we must specify the behaviors that define them.

UNDERSTANDING: PROBLEM SOLVING
AND CONCEPT FORMATION

The term "understanding" is used to refer both to problem-solving skills and to concept formation. Wertheimer, in *Productive Thinking,* gives a precise example of how understanding in the problem-solving sense differs from rote memory. Students are learning to find the area of a parallelogram. Some get a typical problem right. But of those who correctly solve the problem, Wertheimer says, only some "understand" how to find area; the rest are just blindly applying rules. Which students are which? To find out, you give a parallelogram in an unfamiliar position—for example, vertical (see Figure I) instead of horizontal—and ask the students to find its area. Those who convert the new, unfamiliar problem to a familiar problem (for example, by turning the paper sideways) show understanding.

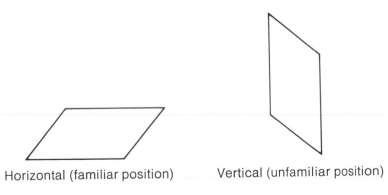

Horizontal (familiar position)   Vertical (unfamiliar position)

Figure I

The example is a good one. The evidence we accept as showing "understanding" is responding correctly in new situations. If, following a lesson on finding areas using parallelograms, a student can find the area of triangles and other areas, we say he "understands" how to find areas. It is not a matter of following rules or not following rules, as Wertheimer states, but of *which* rules are followed. In his example of good teaching, Wertheimer has a rule too. He teaches area by drawing in unit squares (see Figure IIa). His rule is "convert the figure to a

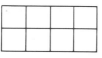

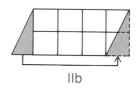

IIa   IIb

Figure II

rectangular form [see Figure IIb] and count the unit squares." The difference between Wertheimer's rule and the rule "multiply the base by the height" lies in the greater transfer value of the former. Wertheimer's rule applies to triangles and other figures as well as parallelograms, whereas the "base times height" rule does not.

The kind of "understanding" Wertheimer describes is understanding of a method or process used in solving problems. There is another kind of understanding called concept formation. It is what we mean when we ask if someone understands the meaning of a word, and it is at the heart of our ability to communicate.

Most words are concepts. Common nouns such as "foot" or "force," adjectives such as "red" or "ionized," and adverbs such as "quickly" or "artistically" are all concepts that exist independently of any particular instance of them.

The degree of understanding of a concept depends on the extent to which we respond to the relevant characteristics of any specific instance of it. In the concept "red," for example, the relevant characteristic is the color. But any specific red object, such as a red coat, also has shape, texture, brightness, size, and so on. A young child may be able to call his coat and ball "red" without being able to call unfamiliar red objects "red." In this case he has learned to say "red" to the question "What color is this?" but he is responding to his coat or ball and not to their color. We can say that he "understands" or "abstracts" the *concept* of color when he responds, not just to the examples used in teaching, but to any unfamiliar example that has the relevant characteristic of redness.

Just as "understanding" in the problem-solving sense involves transfer to new situations, so does understanding a concept. Objectives can be written that require responding to a variety of new situations. The difference between a behavioral objective that is tied to specific cases and one that emphasizes "understanding" in the sense of transfer is shown by the following pairs of objectives.

Objectives
1. The student will be able to calculate the area of a parallelogram given its base and height measurements.
2. The student will be able to calculate or estimate the area of any flat figure in any position, whether or not he has encountered it before, given either its dimensions or a ruler with which to find them.
3. The child will be able to name the color of his red coat and red ball.
4. The child will be able to name the color of unfamiliar red objects differing in size, shape, texture, and brightness.

In objectives 1 and 3 there is no way of determining from correct student behavior whether the child "understands" the concepts of "area" or "red" or whether he has simply memorized correct solutions for these particular problems. The second and fourth objectives, in contrast, specify types of problems or objects that differ from the ones used during instruction. The only way the child can meet the objectives is by responding to the relevant characteristics of "area" and "color" with what we call "understanding."

The problem-solving skills and concepts we teach are part of our scientific and cultural heritage. They are what past generations have found useful. But in order to survive, a culture must change, and its members must not only transmit to new generations the wisdom of the past, but also develop new solutions, new concepts. In addition to problem-solving skills and "understanding" of concepts, education of the young must include skills for creating or discovering new procedures or products.

CREATIVITY

It is often difficult to determine what we mean when we talk of creativity. One characteristic of creative behavior is uniqueness, and we can write objectives that require the student to produce something different from products of others. Being different does not, however, necessarily mean being creative. The teacher who has given students an assignment to write a story is not happy with the child who hands in a paper with only the words "Ho Hum" written on it, even if it is different from all the others. A creative response must meet certain criteria.

Relevant criteria are of two kinds. They may specify the techniques by which a product is to be made, or they may specify the content or function of a product. Thus, in art an objective might be to paint a picture within structural rules referring to balance of light and dark (techniques) or to produce an illusion of depth without using converging lines (content).

TECHNIQUES

In mastering the techniques in a field, the student gains control over his environment in what we call development of skill. Rules will help an individual, for example, make a strong joint in a wooden product or build to a strong climax in a play. They will even help him "express himself." To "express himself," a violinist must be free from having to figure out which finger goes where for each note. Similarly, a student who must concentrate on where to put capital letters and periods cannot express himself as fully as he could without such concern. Rules, conventions, and techniques, when mastered, free the individual from the mechanics of production so that he can concentrate on the message or function of his product.

But, you say, don't great artists break the rules? Yes, they do. A great artist may break rules, but he does not do so out of ignorance of them. When e. e. cummings wrote without using capital letters, it was not because he did not know where they normally go. A rule may occasionally be broken in order to follow another rule, or whole systems of conventions may be thrown out to stimulate new behavior. When an artist breaks with convention, he is restricting his behavior as much as freeing it, for he is not allowing himself to respond in ways that come easy to him. He must produce something new, different not only from products of others, but also from products of his own past. When the twelve-tone composers threw out the conventions of tonality and imposed stringent rules (such as that every one of the twelve tones of the scale must be used before one is repeated), they could no longer produce music that sounded like Mozart's or Brahms'. Breaking the rules made them create new sounds and new solutions to musical problems. In a similar fashion, by rejecting photographic realism, or in using new materials or methods of painting, an artist produces new behavior in himself. Of course, he must still judge which of the novel results are good and which are poor. Not any jumble of notes or drops of paint is successful just because it is different. Some will "work," some not, and the artist is likely to discover procedures that tend to make a good product. These then become new procedural rules that will help the novice work effectively in the new medium.

CONTENT

Although skills in the techniques of production may permit greater freedom for creating, they should not be confused with the content or creative expression itself. Both are needed, and to be sure that both are represented, they should be separate objectives, measured independently. The teacher who asks for a poem in sonnet form is encouraging students to be creative, but if he then grades the papers solely on proper number of lines or rhymes, he is likely to discourage the student who may have poor facility in those skills but who is otherwise possibly quite creative. By having two objectives, one on form and one on content, and by grading some papers on one and some on the other, both writing skills and originality of expression can be developed.

Setting criteria for techniques is a relatively simple matter compared with setting criteria for content or function. It is hard to specify, for example, just what it is that makes a painting beautiful or a story great. By visualizing a very good product and a very bad one and seeing how they differ, however, some of the criteria can be put into words. The art teacher might think of characteristics that made his students' poorer works ineffective. He might remember, for example, a student who intended to convey the idea of the city as a prison, but failed to achieve the desired bar-like effect in the buildings because he tried also to show the city as a place of opposites — dirt and cleanliness, poverty and luxury, bustle and calm. Too many ideas, too many centers of interest overloaded with symbols and details, spoiled the impact of the picture. From this student's problem the teacher could formulate some criteria:

1. A picture should have only one main message and no more than two centers of interest.
2. Symbolism and details should support the main idea of the picture.

The same teacher might also remember his comments on "The Musician," a picture that satisfied the above criteria but was still not successful. The student had made a mosaic using a dark flesh color for the face and hands and a brown color for hair and mandolin. The figure was against a background of darkish smokey greens. What hit the eye, however, was not the face, which was very well done, but the brilliant yellow of the musician's pants and the detail of his red sash. The teacher had pointed out what could be criterion 3:

3. The brightest or most contrasting colors and the sharpest and most intricate detail will normally draw the eye and should therefore be used in the important parts of the picture.

An artist might wish to make a point by brightly coloring and defining trivial details, deliberately obscuring what we normally consider important, but then the trivia becomes the message. This was not the intent of "The Musician."

It is, of course, impossible to outline in advance all of the desirable characteristics of a product that is supposed to differ from others, but many characteristics can be specified. As the teacher works with students, he discovers problem areas and can add new criteria, or principles, for content. The more the criteria are expanded, the more help the teacher gives the student in improving his creative responses.

In some fields the "content" of a product is its function for some purpose. The criteria, in this case, can be stated as a problem. In teaching architecture, for example, a teacher can require creative responses from his students by setting the criteria as a problem to solve. One such teacher assigned a problem in which the students were to design a paper harness and parachute that would safely carry raw eggs dropped from a height of 5 feet to the floor. The task was to make the contraption as light as possible, and a maximum allowable weight was given. To solve the problem, students had to use principles about strength of angles and joints, air resistance, weight and strength of materials, and so on. The test of the quality of the product was the weight of the product and the state of Humpty Dumpty after his ride. (Needless to say, there was a sharp rise in local sales of eggs.)

Objectives for creative responding, in sum, must require novelty within certain limits. To insure novelty, an objective can require a student to produce his own unique product, and can specifically disallow copying. Criteria for the product (in addition to being different from others) can be stated as procedural rules or techniques to be used in the process of creating, as guidelines for content, or as a problem stating the product's function and the specifications to which it must conform.

BLOOM'S TAXONOMY OF EDUCATIONAL OBJECTIVES

It is hard to write objectives specifying the kinds of skills that make up "understanding" or "creativity." They are likely to be omitted or overwhelmed by large numbers of easy-to-write objectives requiring memorized responses.

One attempt to ensure that ample high-quality objectives are represented is *A Taxonomy of Educational Objectives* (Bloom, et al.).

Major Categories of Bloom's Taxonomy

Knowledge
Comprehension } Understanding
Application } Concept Formation
Analysis

Synthesis } Creativity
Evaluation

Figure III

The taxonomy has six main categories within the "cognitive domain." The kinds of skills that make up "understanding" and "concept formation" are classified in four categories (see Figure III); skills that involve creativity fall under "synthesis" and "evaluation."

Bloom and his colleagues do not define their categories behaviorally, but the examples of objectives and test items they give can be used to determine the kinds of behaviors required at each level.

Knowledge

Knowledge is what we normally call "rote memory." The student reproduces a response in the same form as it was presented to him. Common objectives in this category are stating definitions verbatim ("The student will be able to define 'intersection' as the 'common member of two or more sets'"), stating specific facts ("The student will be able to tell the year in which Columbus crossed the Atlantic Ocean to America"), and stating rules ("The student will be able to write the three criteria for a behavioral objective as given in Chapter 3 of this book").

Comprehension

An objective in this category requires the student either to restate or identify restatements of information presented in written or pictorial form. It includes paraphrasing, answering simple questions on information explicitly presented in a paragraph, chart, or graph, summarizing a statement, and translating from one language to another.

Application

Application closely parallels Wertheimer's definition of "understanding" in that the student must solve problems that differ from ones he has seen before. Solving problems that are virtually identical to familiar ones (for example, a mathematics word problem with different numbers but essentially the same words) is not "application" but "knowledge," because the student could be responding to characteristics of the specific example and not to the relevant concepts.

Analysis

In an analysis objective, the student must identify the component parts or structure of a whole. He might, for example, diagram the basic form of a work of art such as a play or symphony. He might isolate the basic parts of an object or organism and explain their relationship to each other. He might trace the development of a particular concept, style, or pattern of behavior, pulling out those aspects of history that support his viewpoint. As in the application objective, the specific example the student analyzes must be sufficiently different from any he has seen analyzed before to make sure that he cannot supply its form or structure by rote memory. The reproduction of a memorized analysis is, of course, a skill at the knowledge level.

Synthesis

Synthesis includes those objectives in which the student must combine elements to make a unique product. Because, in synthesis, the student must express his *own* ideas and experiences, the product of each student will differ from the products of others. A school room in which thirty identical pictures of Halloween pumpkins hang like reflections in a double-mirror shows knowledge not synthesis, even though each student cut out his own triangular eyes and glued on his own green stem bent to the left.

Evaluation

In evaluation, the student tells whether or not a given product meets specified criteria or compares two products for some purpose and gives his reasoning. To be evaluation and not comprehension or application, the objective must require expression of an individual viewpoint. There must be no single "right answer." "To select the best examples of capitalism from a list of governments," for instance, is comprehension, not evaluation, because to meet this objective, the student must "understand" the concept of capitalism but need not express his own ideas. Similarly, "to use some criteria to choose the best of several products" is not evaluation unless a number of them could be rightfully chosen and the student is also required to provide the rationale for his particular choice. In an evaluation objective, in other words, there must also be some synthesis.

USE OF THE TAXONOMY

It is easy to write objectives at the knowledge level of Bloom's taxonomy, and they are the foundation upon which disciplines are built. Unless we incorporate the higher levels too, however, we shall not be teaching the behaviors that make up understanding, concept formation, and creativity.

Just by classifying the objectives for a unit of instruction, we become aware of the number of each kind of objective we have included. In writing objectives for the areas that are underrepresented, we are likely to create new objectives that will promote understanding, concept formation, and creativity. An example of a unit improved by such a process follows:

Music: Unit on Reading Rhythms

Level: *Objective:*

Knowledge   To name the following notes: ♩, ♩, ♩, ♩, ♩.

Knowledge   To tell how many quarter notes equal a whole note and a half note in length (that is, 𝅝 = 𝅘𝅥 𝅘𝅥 𝅘𝅥 𝅘𝅥; 𝅗𝅥 = 𝅘𝅥 𝅘𝅥).

Knowledge   To match whole, half, quarter, and sixteenth notes with their equivalent rests (𝅝 = ▬; 𝅗𝅥 = ▄; and so forth.)

Knowledge   To tell how many of what kind of notes belong in a measure with the following time signatures: 4/4, 3/4, 6/8.

The point of the unit above, according to its title, is reading rhythms. Instead of just memorizing names and values of notes and rests (objectives l through 3), the student should use these values to read rhythms. Knowing that a quarter rest takes as long as a quarter note is not very helpful in clapping a measure that may take a second or two to go by. For most purposes the measure 𝅘𝅥 𝅘𝅥𝅘𝅥 is the same as 𝅘𝅥 𝅘𝅥 𝅘𝅥 ♩. (Both have the rhythm of the word "anyhow"). Just as the reader would pronounce "phess" like "fes" without stopping to verbalize "ph sounds like f, and ss sounds like s," the reader of rhythms must react to the whole pattern and not to the individual notes.

The objectives above were revised accordingly:

Revised Unit

Knowledge   1. To clap any combination of two or more of the following five measures at a speed of one measure every three seconds.

| 𝅗𝅥 𝅗𝅥 | 𝅗𝅥 𝅘𝅥 𝅘𝅥 | 𝅘𝅥 𝅘𝅥 𝅗𝅥 | 𝅘𝅥 𝅘𝅥 𝅘𝅥 𝅘𝅥 | 𝅝 |

Knowledge   2. To write notes for any measure of rhythm he hears (using the rhythms above).

Comprehension   3. To clap the next measure in a pattern he hears or sees written on paper (that is,

𝅗𝅥 𝅘𝅥 𝅘𝅥 |𝅗𝅥 𝅘𝅥 𝅘𝅥 |𝅗𝅥 𝅘𝅥 𝅘𝅥 |−|). (*Note:* This is similar to supplying the missing words in a sentence—for example, "He brushed his teeth, put on his pajamas, and went to ____"—and involves "understanding" to the degree of "completing to make sense.")

Application

4. To add notes to correctly complete a measure of 4/4.

Synthesis

5. To make up and clap his own four-measure phrase (using any combination of the four measures above) so that it "comes to rest" at the end.

Evaluation

6. To tell which of a number of five to ten measure rhythms best conveys a feeling (such as joy or sadness) and to defend his choice (there is no one right answer).

8

Writing Worthwhile Objectives

Pretest

Directions: Take this pretest and score it. (Directions for scoring are at the end of the test.) If you score 90 percent or better, proceed to Chapter 9; otherwise, do the exercises in Chapter 8 for the parts you missed.

Part I

Directions: Next to each objective below write the number of the highest category of Bloom's Taxonomy in which the objective falls using:

1 for knowledge   4 for analysis
2 for comprehension   5 for synthesis
3 for application   6 for evaluation

_____ 1. Given an unknown contemporary piece of music, the student will write an essay on the quality of the orchestration using as criteria the principles outlined in the orchestration text.

_____ 2. To list at least five of the six local community organizations for health maintenance covered in the course.

_____ 3. To state the following applications of Boyle's Law (list of applications would follow).

_____ 4. To write an original fable using the moral of one of Aesop's *Fables.*

_____ 5. To be able to pronounce ten new sight words that follow the silent "e" rule.

_____ 6. To answer simple questions on information presented in bar, circle, and line graphs. (The questions will require only straight "reading" of the graphs; no figuring will be necessary.)

_____ 7. To write humorous words to fit the tune "Red River

Valley." The words should scan and rhyme as in the original song.

_____ 8. To give an example of the concept of "freedom of speech" from the student's own personal experience.

_____ 9. To choose the best "topic sentence" in a paragraph at the tenth-grade reading level.

_____10. Given an educational problem in question form, select the best of the following experimental designs to answer the question (list of experimental designs would follow).

_____11. To state the three main products of Brazil.

_____12. To use the recommended method of artificial respiration for any possible situation requiring such treatment.

Part II

Directions: Under each knowledge-level objective below, write an objective that requires the student to use, rather than just memorize, the information, rule, or principle.

Sample

To state the three steps in locating a given book in the library (according to the text).

To locate a book in the library within five minutes, given its title and author (using the three steps discussed in the text).

---

1. To list the following requirements for a behavioral objective.

a. They refer to the behavior of the student.
b. (Rest of list would follow.)

2. To define the following:
    a. Totalitarianism—absolute control by a highly central-ized government permitting no difference of political opinion
    b. Democracy—government by the people through freely elected representatives
    c. Anarchy—a state of society without government or law

3. To state that, in general, the smaller the animal the faster its heart will beat.

4. State the steps listed in the text for inserting paper into the typewriter for an original copy and one carbon.

Part I: *Directions for Scoring*
Score 1 point for each correct answer.

Answers
  1. 6
  2. 1

3. 1. Stating applications involves rote memorization. The student is not applying Boyle's Law himself.
4. 5
5. 3
6. 2
7. 5
8. 2. Giving an original example of a concept is an extension for single words or phrases of the process of paraphrasing.
9. 2
10. 3. The student is *applying* principles about the suitability of experimental designs for given problems. Although some evaluation is involved in deciding which designs are appropriate, the student is not evaluating in the sense of pointing out strengths and weaknesses.
11. 1
12. 3

If you missed any of these, see Exercises 1, 2, and 3.

Part II: *Directions for Scoring*
Sample objectives are listed below. Score 2 points if your objective is most like the "best" objectives, 1 point if it is like the "acceptable" objectives, and zero points if it is like the "unacceptable" objectives.

1. Best (score 2 points)
   To mark (or otherwise identify) the behavioral objectives in a list of objectives.
   To write behavioral objectives meeting the three requirements.
   To tell which requirement a given objective meets or fails to meet.

For each requirement for a behavioral objective, to write two sample objectives—one that meets the requirement, one that does not.

Acceptable (score 1 point)
To state in your own words the meaning of each requirement.
To tell why an objective should be behavioral (this is really on a different topic).

Unacceptable (score 0 points)
To write the requirements.
To state the requirements.
Or
Any objective in which the student reproduces the three requirements.

2. Best (score 2 points)
To classify given unfamiliar social systems (either existing ones or descriptions of fictitious ones) as totalitarian, democratic, or anarchistic (using ones not discussed in class or in assignments).
To write (or select) statements on how totalitarianism, democracy, and anarchy affect people in areas of daily life such as getting news, schooling of children, security against housebreaking, and so forth.
To describe how your life would change if our country suddenly became totalitarian or anarchistic.
To write a story in which at least five events or actions show whether the hero lives in a democratic, totalitarian, or anarchistic regime.

Acceptable (score 1 point)
To outline in your own words some advantages and disadvantages of each form of government.
To define totalitarianism, democracy, and anarchy in your own words.

Unacceptable (score 0 points)
To state that totalitarianism is absolute control by a highly centralized government . . . (and so forth).
To orally define totalitarianism as the absolute control by a highly centralized government . . . (and so forth).

3. Best (score 2 points)
To tell which of two or more animals of different sizes will have the fastest heart beat, or to number animals (whose relative sizes the student would know) by speed of heart beat.
With a given pulse rate as a standard, to select or tell whether a faster or slower pulse would probably be normal or indicative of illness in given animals. (For example, if John, age seven, found a chipmunk and noticed its heart was beating much faster than his, would this indicate illness in the chipmunk? Why or why not?)
To give an original example of an animal that would have a faster or slower heart beat than a given animal.

Acceptable (score 1 point)
To state in your own words that, in general, the smaller the animal the faster its heart will beat.

Unacceptable (score 0 points)
To write, tell, or mark as true, the statement that the smaller the animal the faster its heart will beat.

4. Best (score 2 points)
To insert paper into a typewriter for an original and one carbon. (You may wish to add "following the steps listed in the text.")

Acceptable (score 1 point)
To type an original and one carbon. (This is really more than just inserting paper.)
To apply the steps for inserting paper. (It is better to tell

what the student will be doing when he is "applying the steps.")

Unacceptable (score 0 points)
Any objective that requires talking or writing about inserting paper.

If you missed any of these, see Exercise 4.

(Total possible points = 20.)

In knowledge objectives, the student reproduces, with little or no change, what was presented to him. Such objectives can be learned by rote memory with little or no "understanding" of what is repeated. The lack of understanding is illustrated by the kindergarten child who was painting a picture for "Silent Night."

Silent Night, Holy Night.
All is calm. All is bright.
'Round yon' Virgin, Mother and child,
Holy infant so tender and mild.
Sleep in heavenly peace,
Sleep in heavenly peace.

There was Mary, babe, and a fat little man. Asked who he was, the child replied, "That's Round John Virgin." Teachers who ask children to write the Pledge of Allegiance for the first time can often see a similar lack of "understanding."

Even if an objective is to repeat an application, a particular analysis, or someone's evaluation of something, it does not qualify for the higher categories but is still knowledge.

Directions: Check the knowledge objectives in the list below.

_____ 1. The student will be able to list the three applications of the steam engine as discussed in class.
_____ 2. To spell correctly at least 80 percent of the words in the sixth-grade speller.
_____ 3. To write an original poem of six lines.
_____ 4. To outline the three main points in Shaw's evaluation of English spelling.
_____ 5. To define "behavioral objectives" in your own words.
_____ 6. To give three examples, not used in class or readings, showing that a society's architecture is formed partly by the materials in its environment.

_____ 7. To sing "Jingle Bells" from memory (no accompaniment).

_____ 8. To make up a tune for "Old Mother Hubbard" that starts and ends on the same note.

_____ 9. Given three new stories, to tell which one best follows chronological development, and show where the other two fail.

_____10. To find the area of unfamiliar figures made only of right angles and straight lines.

Answers

Knowledge objectives are numbers 1, 2, 4, and 7. Number 5, while requiring the student to define a word, specifies that he is to use his own words. To do that, he must paraphrase, a skill classified in "understanding." Number 6 involves giving examples and is also comprehension. New examples ("not used in class or readings") cannot be given by rote learning alone.

Each category in Bloom's list builds upon skills from the ones below it. For the comprehension level, the student must not only repeat, but must "understand" what he has learned at least well enough to paraphrase it or state it in another form. Translating from one language (such as French) into another, or stating in words information that is presented in a picture or graph, is a special kind of paraphrasing and is also comprehension.

When dealing with a concept such as "red" or "behavioral objective," a comprehension-level objective is likely to require the student to give his own examples of the concept or to tell whether or not the concept applies to new examples. If a kindergarten child can name or point to something that is red in addition to the objects used to teach "red," and if he can tell whether or not a given object is red, we say he "comprehends" the concept of "red."

Directions: Check the comprehension objectives in the following list.

_____ 1. To recite the poem "The Oak Tree."
_____ 2. To tell in one sentence the meaning of the poem "The Oak Tree."
_____ 3. To recite the English translation of the French song "Frère Jacques."
_____ 4. To translate a sentence (similar to those in the text) from Spanish into English.
_____ 5. Using a circle graph showing information (such as the exports of various countries), to answer simple comparative questions (such as which countries export more or less of a given product than other countries).
_____ 6. To give an original example of "sarcasm."

_____ 7. To underline all the verbs in a new list of words.

_____ 8. To write the sum of two-digit numbers, at a rate of at least six correct per minute.

_____ 9. To point at five "containers" in the class (excluding ones used while teaching the meaning of the word).

_____10. To touch his "right" or "left" knee, ear, foot, and so forth.

Answers

Comprehension objectives are numbers 2, 4, 5, 6, 7, 9 (pointing out containers is a way of giving examples), and 10 ("touch your left ear" is essentially giving an example of the concept "left"). Number 3, although about the English translation of a French song, does not require the student to translate but rather to recite from memory. It is a knowledge-level objective.

In an application objective, the student is required to use a method, rule, or principle to solve a problem. The problem must be new. If it is not, the student may be memorizing solutions, not applying the principles. Take, for example, the rule "silent 'e' makes the preceding vowel long." Just because a child can pronounce "like," "make," "hope," and "Pete" does not mean that he is applying the silent "e" rule, for he may have memorized those words as "sight" vocabulary. If he correctly pronounces "pake," however, or other nonsense syllables with silent "e," we feel confident that he is applying the rule, because he is not likely to have memorized those particular examples. Because the reason for learning a rule is to help with unfamiliar or new situations, not those we already know, it is important that we teach skills at the application level.

Directions: Next to each objective below, write K if it is a knowledge objective, A if it is an application objective.

_____1. To apply the silent "e" rule in pronouncing the following familiar words: cake, bike, dope, skate, and white.

_____2. To pronounce unfamiliar words or nonsense syllables (such as sike) the follow the silent "e" rule.

_____3. To locate the malfunction in a radio using the troubleshooting tests discussed in class (the radios and malfunctions will *not* be those used as examples during training).

_____4. Using trigonometry, to calculate the distance between any two specified objects on the school grounds or the height of any given object around school.

_____5. To use the principles of setting up a letter in typing the letter on page 60 of the typing text.

DISTINGUISHING BETWEEN APPLICATION, COMPREHENSION, AND EVALUATION

An objective may use the word "apply" without being an application objective. We have already seen how "applying" a rule to recite familiar examples requires only knowledge. In a similar way, if what is applied is not a principle or procedure, but a *concept,* the skills involved are more appropriately classified as "comprehension." To "apply" the concept of "free enterprise," we must refer to specific examples of economic systems. Identifying or giving examples, however, is a comprehension-level skill.

For an application objective, the student would have to apply some *principles* of "free enterprise" to solve a problem. He could, for example, outline a law that would solve a given violation of free enterprise, or tell how a given condition of supply and demand would affect the price of an article under a free enterprise system. We cannot, in short, *apply* a concept in the sense of "application" outlined here. It is only when the student uses a principle, rule, or procedure that an objective is classified as "application."

Occasionally, the word "apply" will occur in an evaluation objective. Although to evaluate we must apply standards, an evaluation objective must also include skills from the analysis or synthesis levels. The student must apply criteria, analyze, and express his own particular viewpoint or reasoning. If these are not present, then the objective is application. "Choosing the best product according to given standards," for example, would be classified as "application," because it does not involve any verbal reasoning. "Choosing the 'best' product and defending the choice according to some criteria," would be an evaluation objective. Because the uniqueness of a point of view is important in evaluation objectives, they cannot be adequately met by multiple-choice exercises. In contrast, multiple-choice exercises can be used to measure application-level skills.

Directions: Indicate the level of each objective below by writing

K for knowledge
C for comprehension
A for application
   or
E for evaluation

_____ 6. To conduct a group discussion according to principles of democratic group action (after discussing other examples of the process).

_____ 7. To give an original example of "triangle trade" (using, for example, local towns instead of the thirteen colonies, Cuba, and England).

_____ 8. To write the three applications of the principles of scientific control discussed in class.

_____ 9. To indicate how a particular piece of home-remedy folk lore would affect the health of a given community and why.

_____10. To take a blood sample and obtain the blood type, hemoglobin content, and Rh factor, using standard laboratory procedures.

Answers
  1. K. The rule is not being applied to *new* or *unfamiliar* words.
  2. A.
  3. A.
  4. A. Specifying "any two objects" or "any given object" implies that the student must be able to use the procedure in situations he has not previously encountered. We would

not expect him to be able to memorize all possible examples.

5. K. Restricting the typing to one particular letter gives this away as knowledge.
6. A. The principles are being applied to a new situation.
7. C. Giving examples is not applying a principle, rule, or procedure. It is "comprehending" a *concept*.
8. K.
9. E. The student is being asked to judge the value of a folk remedy according to the standard of "health of a given community." To do it he must analyze the remedy and the alternatives and draw a conclusion.
10. A. This is application of methods of blood analysis.

The category of "analysis" includes objectives that require the identification of structural parts of a whole. An analysis objective in psychology might be to identify relevant components in a narrative case history. The student might be asked, for example, to pinpoint a child's problem in terms of behavior, and identify likely causes for the behavior from the information given. To give such an analysis, the student must use skills in previous categories. He must "know" what to look for, he must "comprehend" the concepts involved, and he must "apply" the principles to the unfamiliar case history. Because the emphasis is on breaking down the whole into parts, however, the task is principally one of analysis.

When a student must design and create an original product, he has reached the level of synthesis. In the categories below synthesis, there is often a single right or best answer. In contrast, for synthesis, each student must express his own ideas, experiences, or viewpoint, and there is no one right answer. Any product that measures up to the standards of workmanship and embodies the student's own creative expression meets the objective.

Directions: For each objective below, write S for synthesis, A for analysis, or N for neither.

_____1. To complete a story that will make sense out of an unusual situation presented in the first three to five sentences given.

_____2. To diagram the structure of a classical string quartet identifying, if present, major and minor themes, major key changes, bridge passages, development, and coda.

_____3. To make your own Halloween mask out of a paper bag. The mask must be designed so that you can see out and it must have at least one moving part controlled by a string you can pull while wearing the mask.

____4. To give an original example of "acceleration."

____5. To define "compound" in your own words.

Answers

1. S. Although restrictions are imposed, the student is asked to create. This kind of objective will produce a wide variety of stories.
2. A. This is a typical example of the analysis of musical compositions.
3. S.
4. N. Giving an example is comprehension. Even though the students' products will be different, the objective is to *understand* the concept of "acceleration," not to create something. The objective could be met by listing various processes and, in a multiple-choice fashion, picking one that is acceleration. It is an extension of the comprehension objective, "give a list of situations, mark those that are examples of acceleration."
5. N. It is comprehension, even though there will be variation in the products.

An evaluation objective should include skills from the preceding five categories. It differs from applying standards (for instance, telling which of a number of headlines meets certain criteria) in that it must include the student's own viewpoint or judgement. An evaluation item might be "to tell which of a number of headlines would be best for given situations (for example, attracting attention in a student newspaper) and defend your choice."

The individuality in evaluation does not lie in choosing among alternatives, but in the reasoning involved and in the selection of evidence to back up the position taken. Because individual expression is an essential ingredient of evaluation, it, like synthesis, cannot be adequately tested by multiple-choice items.

Directions: Indicate the level of each objective below by writing

1 for knowledge
2 for comprehension
3 for application
4 for analysis
5 for synthesis
6 for evaluation

_____ 1. To make the A-frame bird feeder on page 10 of the shop handbook following the steps outlined. (The feeder must also satisfy class criteria of good workmanship.)

_____ 2. To design and build an original bird feeder that will keep seed dry in a rain storm with high winds. (Standard models are not acceptable.)

_____ 3. To tell which of a number of bird feeders is best according to the standards for "squirrel proofing" discussed in class.

_____ 4. To tell which counseling treatment would most benefit a student and give reasoning, given the student's case history, relevant test scores, and teachers' reports.

_____ 5. To use the "toothpick test" to determine which of several different cakes are done and which need further baking.

_____ 6. To criticize a research study on the appropriateness of statistical methods for the problem selected, using the text as reference.

_____ 7. To design and construct a poster to communicate at least two of your views on school rules concerning dress.

_____ 8. To trace the main theme and secondary theme of a play such as one by Shakespeare, citing the characters involved, the conflicts and allegiances, and the way in which the themes are developed.

_____ 9. To give an example, from your own experience, of "authoritarianism."

_____10. To define "electromagnet" as "a device consisting of an iron or steel core that is magnetized by electric current in a coil that surrounds it."

Answers

  1. 3. Following directions is an application of rules.
  2. 5
  3. 3. This is an example of applying standards where there is a right and wrong answer, and no personal viewpoint is required.
  4. 6
  5. 3. The cakes should not be those used during instruction.

Each cake tested in this case is a new situation with its own characteristics in which the procedure is to be applied.

6. 6. Different positions could be taken, depending upon personal preferences on practicality, purity of design, or amount and kinds of information desired.
7. 5
8. 4
9. 2
10. 1

Exercise 6
The Alternatives to Knowledge Objectives

It is easy to write "knowledge" objectives. Without realizing it, a teacher may design a unit, most of which requires the student to memorize information. Because these objectives alone do not capture what is worthwhile or useful in a subject area (see Chapter 7), they should whenever possible be rewritten to incorporate more relevant skills. Instead of requiring our students to repeat content verbatim, we can ask them to use it. Some common forms of knowledge objectives follow with some sample ways to revise them to incorporate more worthwhile skills.

TO DEFINE

Instead of just asking for a definition of a term or concept, we can require the student to use it in some way. Some alternatives to "define" are given below with an example from chemistry.

> Knowledge objective: "To define 'compound' as 'a pure substance that is composed of two or more elements and whose composition is constant.'"

Taxonomic Category	Alternative Skills	Examples
Comprehension	1. To tell in your own words what the term means.	1. To tell in your own words what a "compound" is.
Comprehension	2. To identify instances and noninstances of the concept (using ones not covered in class).	2. To tell which of several substances are compounds.
Comprehension	3. To given original examples of the concept and noninstances of it (any	3. To name three compounds (other than ones used in class or readings) and

		three substances that are not compounds.
	"application" of concept to concrete examples is "comprehension").	
Synthesis	4. To create a product using the concept.	4. To create a compound (other than ones known to the student) and demonstrate that it is a compound. Or To describe a fictitious compound and tell how it would behave in various tests.

TO STATE A RULE OR PRINCIPLE

The best way to learn a rule or principle is to apply it. If we write an application objective that requires *using* the rule or principle, it is rarely necessary to require memorizing it also. For example, instead of the objective "to state the rule for pronouncing words ending in silent 'e' (a silent 'e' makes the preceding vowel long)," we can substitute the objective "to pronounce unfamiliar words ending in silent 'e'." If we want to make certain that the child is sounding out the words phonetically and not just memorizing silent "e" words individually, we could even write "to pronounce unfamiliar nonsense syllables, such as 'labe,' using the rule for pronouncing words in silent 'e'."

TO LIST REQUIREMENTS OR CRITERIA

Listing requirements or criteria does not guarantee that the student can use them either for creating products of his own (synthesis) or evaluating products of others (evaluation). Yet these are presumably the reason why the requirements or criteria are taught. For example, instead of, or in addition to, learning to state "The four fundamentals of good design are proportion, balance, harmony, and ryhthm," a student could be required to select the better of two designs and tell why it is better in terms of proportion, balance, harmony, and rhythm, or to design something himself that has good proportion, balance, harmony, and rhythm.

Directions: Write an objective at each taxonomic category indicated, in which the student must use the knowledge in the objective given.

1. To define "composite number" as "a whole number that is a multiple of two other numbers, neither of which is 1." Comprehension:

2. To state the rule for forming the present participle of one-syllable words ending in "ie" (for example, tie). Application:

3. To state the following criteria for a good business letter.
   a. It should state the business as briefly as possible without omitting important information.
   b. It should use "formal" English.
   c. It should request ("would it be possible . . .") instead of demand ("I want . . ."). Synthesis:

Evaluation:

4. To state the principle that population centers grow up along routes of transportation and that the geography of a country thus plays an important role in the development of cities.
Application:

Sample Answers
1. Comprehension
To state (tell, outline, and so forth) *in your own words* what a "composite number" is.

Or

To mark the composite numbers in a list of numbers (or any identification of composite numbers).

Or

To give your own example of a composite number.

2. To form the present participate of *new* one-syllable words ending in "ie" (or of nonsense words, words not used during instruction, and so forth). By insisting that the words be new, we make sure that the student is not memorizing the spelling of particular words such as "tying" or "dying," and that when he meets an unfamiliar word such as "vie," he can "use the rule" to form its present participle.

3. Synthesis

To write original business letters that meet the three criteria (either given specific purposes for the letters or with students picking their own).

Evaluation
To tell which of three letters is the best business letter, comparing them on the three criteria (or to evaluate given letters in terms of the three criteria).

4. To draw, on a geographical map of an unfamiliar or fictitious country, places where population centers would be likely to grow (or to select likely and unlikely towns or cities on a geographical map of a fictitious country).

Part I

Directions: Next to each objective below write the number of the highest category of Bloom's Taxonomy in which the objective falls using:

1 for knowledge
2 for comprehension
3 for application
4 for analysis
5 for synthesis
6 for evaluation

_____ 1. To select a written statement that summarizes social data given in table form.

_____ 2. To use the principles of operant conditioning as stated in *How to Train Animals* to train a child to name five colors (the child should know none of them initially).

_____ 3. To state the following rule about electrical charges: Like charges repel each other, unlike charges attract each other.

_____ 4. To collect on the school grounds an example of the following: oak leaf, stamine, pistol, etc.

_____ 5. To write the following definition of "polynomial in one variable": "An expression of the general form $ax^n + bx^{n-1} + \ldots k$, where a, b, and k are any real numbers."

_____ 6. To list the two or three main safety hazards in any home (from slides, pictures, or actual rooms), following the regulations outlined in the text.

_____ 7. To give at least three original examples of things that are "living" and three original examples of things that are "not living."

_____ 8. To identify the following parts of a research report:

stated assumptions, hidden (or unstated) assumptions, and conclusions or generalizations, with the research findings upon which they were based. (Reports used will be similar to those published in journals such as *The Educational Researcher.*)

_____ 9. To list the following applications of compressed air power: pneumatic drills (rest of list would follow).

_____10. Given relevant information in story form for a hypothetical high school student, to criticize his choice of occupation, covering the following points and using facts to back up the point of view taken:
a. short-term gains or losses (social and financial)
b. (rest of list would follow)

_____11. To outline a new procedure for finding the weight of a solid. Procedures similar to the two in the text (balance and compression of a spring) will not be accepted.

_____12. To tell in one's own words a story read in the reader, including the four or five main events in correct chronological order.

Part II

Directions: Under each knowledge-level objective below, write an objective that requires the student to use, rather than just memorize, the information, rule, or principle.

Sample

To state the three steps in locating a given book in the library (according to the text).

To locate a book in the library within five minutes, given its title and author (using the three steps discussed in the text).

---

1. To list the following requirements for a paragraph.
   a. A paragraph should be made up of complete sentences.
   b. A paragraph must have only one main idea or topic.
   c. Each sentence must be on the topic.

2. To write the equation for finding the density of a block of material.

3. To define vertebrate as an animal that has a backbone or spinal column.

4. To state the rule for forming a negative reply in Spanish.

Part I: *Directions for Scoring*
Score 1 point for each correct answer.

Answers: 1–2, 2–3, 3–1, 4–2, 5–1, 6–3, 7–2, 8–4, 9–1, 10–6, 11–5, 12–2

Part II: *Directions for Scoring*
Sample objectives are below. Score two points if your objective is most like the "best" objectives, one point if it is like the "ac-

ceptable" objectives, and zero points if it is like the unacceptable objectives.

1. Best (score 2 points)
   To mark (or otherwise identify) groups of words that make an acceptable paragraph and ones that do not.
   To pick the better of two paragraphs (according to the criteria).
   To tell which requirements a given paragraph meets or fails.
   To edit a paragraph to make it meet the requirements.
   To write a paragraph that meets the requirements.

   Acceptable (score 1 point)
   To tell in the student's own words what makes a good paragraph.
   To tell the meaning of each requirement.

   Unacceptable (score 0 points)
   Any objective in which the student's product is producing the three requirements.

2. Best (score 2 points)
   To find (calculate, and so forth) the density of any block of material given the necessary information about the block (and the equation).

   Acceptable (score 1 point)
   To tell how you would find the density of a block of material.
   To tell what each of the letters means in the equation for finding density.

   Unacceptable (score 0 points)
   Writing or selecting the correct formula.

3. Best (score 2 points)
   To classify unfamiliar animals (from drawings or descriptions of relevant bone structures) as vertebrate or invertebrate.

To classify unfamiliar bone structures or models of bone structures as coming from a vertebrate or from an invertebrate animal.

To draw a fictitious vertebrate with a tracing paper overlay showing his skeletal structure (must be adequate for his size and weight).

To judge whether or not a given classification of an unfamiliar animal as vertebrate or not was correct and tell why or why not.

Acceptable (score 1 point)
To tell what a vertebrate is in your own words.

Unacceptable (score 0 points)
To produce or mark the correct definition.

4. Best (score 2 points)
To reply negatively in Spanish to questions similar to, but not identical to, ones in Chapter X of the text (orally or in writing).

To write, or give orally, Spanish translations of negative replies given in English (using ones not encountered in the text).

To select the correct negative Spanish reply (using ones not previously seen).

Acceptable (score 1 point)
To tell in your own words how to form a negative reply in Spanish.

Unacceptable (score 0 points)
To write, recite, or mark, or otherwise reproduce the rule on forming a negative reply in Spanish.

9

Developing a Unit

There is no pretest for Chapter 9. The chapter contains a number of suggestions (with exercises) for ways in which to go about writing objectives for a unit that will utilize a given textbook.

The posttest for Chapter 9 is to write objectives for a unit using one of the sample textbook chapters provided, or, preferably, a chapter from a textbook you plan to use in teaching. You may procede to write your unit now (see page 160 for directions), turning back to the exercises as needed, or do whatever exercises you feel will be useful first and then write your posttest unit.

Exercise 1 Finding the Objectives
for a Textbook Chapter, or "How Do We Begin?"

Most of us are handed a textbook with each teaching assignment, and with the textbook before us we begin designing our course. We ask ourselves the basic question "What skills do I want my students to have when they've finished my course?"

Usually, we can state some general goals. In addition, most textbooks list their basic aims in the front of the teacher's or student's edition. Even when no basic aim is specified as such, goals are likely to be stated in the introduction, foreword, or preface as in the following:

> The *Cambridge Exploration Series* is designed to follow the natural development of interests of the youngster, starting in the first grade with the child's immediate neighborhood which consists of home, school, local stores, and so forth, and gradually expanding through the grades to encompass the whole world. Each book is designed to lead the student through a series of planned experiences which will lead him step by step to a better understanding of the geographical and human world so that he can assume the responsibilities of helping make the world a better place in which to live.

It is helpful to jot down one or two general goals so we can evaluate the relative importance of topics. For example, if one of the general goals for a course in testing for teachers is to teach how to use standardized test results, we should write more objectives on interpreting standardized test results than, say, on the history of the standardized testing movement. If we are using a text that has a separate chapter covering the history of the Stanford Binet, we may be tempted to write a lot of history items. By reminding ourselves of the overall purpose of the course, we can shift our emphasis to the more relevant topics.

BUILDING A UNIT AROUND CONCEPTS

With the general purposes in front of us, we turn to designing individual units. Many teachers find it helpful first to list one or more concepts they wish to get across in each unit. A unit on history might center around the concept of "democracy." A concept in science could be "mass," in mathematics, "addition." To "understand" a concept, in the sense of Chapter 7, the child must be able to (1) tell whether or not a specific new example is an example of the concept, (2) tell why or why not, and (3) give an original example of the concept. For the unit on history the teacher might write the following: (1) "to tell whether or not a fictitious government described in a one-page story is a democracy"; (2) "to tell why a described government is not a democracy (using the criteria in the text)"; (3) "to write a two-page story in which the main character does at least four things that would indicate that his society is democratic," or perhaps "to outline a democratic procedure for running the school lunchroom."

Similar objectives for "mass" and "addition" could be written, for example:

Science
1. To check procedures that would alter the mass of an object from a list such as the following:
   putting a chunk of wood into "weightless" orbit in space
   cooling the wood 3°F
   burning the wood, and so forth.
2. To tell why doing something to a chunk of wood would or would not change its mass.
3. To describe at least two things (not used in class or readings) you could do to an object that would alter its mass and two that would not.

Math

1. To label descriptions of everyday processes as addition or subtraction. (For example, John and Sue each had three apples. They put them all in one bag.)
2. To tell why a given process is or is not addition.
3. To "tell a story about adding" or to "show adding" by putting things together, telling what you are adding to what.

Note that in writing these objectives for a concept, we get above Bloom's knowledge level, and several categories are represented.

USING THE OBJECTIVES IN A TEXTBOOK

Some textbooks list objectives for each unit. Although they are likely to be general, they can be used to derive behavioral objectives. If no objectives are listed, exercises or questions at the end of chapters indicate what is expected of the student. When these too are lacking, we must work from the text. Usually, important concepts or "understandings" are printed in special type or labeled in some way. By asking how we would test the student on these central ideas, we can formulate some behavioral objectives.

Directions: Write one concept and one to three main objectives for each minichapter on the following pages. Space for you to write in is provided on pages 150 and 152.

Teacher's Manual for Minichapter on Length (third grade)

I. Overview

Chapter Four explains the use of the foot ruler and yardstick to measure length.

II. Materials

For measuring you will need a yardstick and a foot ruler.

III. Procedures

Introduce the chapter by holding up the foot ruler and the yardstick and discuss how they are alike and how they are different. Then have the students read the chapter. As a culminating experience, teacher and students should measure objects around the room.

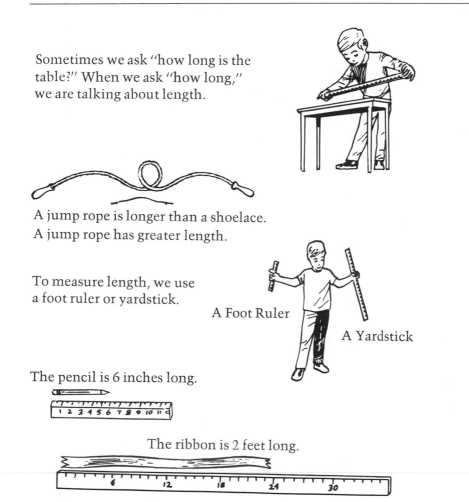

Sometimes we ask "how long is the table?" When we ask "how long," we are talking about length.

A jump rope is longer than a shoelace. A jump rope has greater length.

To measure length, we use a foot ruler or yardstick.

A Foot Ruler

A Yardstick

The pencil is 6 inches long.

The ribbon is 2 feet long.

Questions for Thought
a. Which is longer, the foot ruler or the yardstick? _____
b. How many foot rulers lined up would be as long as one yardstick? _____

149

Objectives

Concept:

Objectives:

Aim: To make every subject and verb agree.

The subject and verb in English sentences must agree in number. If the subject is singular, the verb must also be singular. If the subject is plural, the verb should also be plural.

Correct

She sings well.
/ \
(singular) (singular)

Incorrect

She sing well.
/ \
(singular) (plural)

The plural of a verb does not have an s, but the plural of most nouns is formed by adding s.

	Singular	*Plural*
Verbs:	runs	run
	hits	hit
Nouns:	chair	chairs
	dog	dogs

Watch Out for "Don't"

"Don't" should only be used with a plural subject.

Exercises
1. The girl (draw, draws) beautifully.
2. Girls (draw, draws) well.
3. She (don't, doesn't) have a bicycle.
4. They (don't, doesn't) have bicycles.

151

Objectives
Concept:

Objectives:

First Minichapter: *Sample Answers*
1. A concept that is stressed is "length." To make sure the students "understand" the term, one or more of the following comprehension objectives could be included.
   a. To tell which of several measures indicates length (using standard measures and informal ones, for example, the fisherman's holding out his hands "It was *this* long").
   b. To give his own examples of the length of an object (using his arms, steps paced as standard measures).
2. The overview talks of using a foot ruler and yardstick to measure length, so one objective could be to measure objects of various lengths to the nearest foot with a yardstick, or to the nearest inch with a foot ruler.
3. From the procedure, the following objective could be derived, but it is probably not central to the lesson: To tell two ways in which a foot ruler and a yardstick are alike, and two ways in which they are different (given the actual rulers).

4. An objective for the "Questions for Thought" could be phrased, "To tell how many feet are in a yard and to tell which is longer—a foot ruler or a yardstick."

Second Minichapter: *Sample Answers*
1. From the "Aim," objectives such as the following could be derived.
   a. To edit sentences, writing in the correct verb or subject so that they agree.
   b. To write a composition of 100 words in which all verbs agree with their subjects.
2. Objectives for the exercises are:
   a. To select the form of the verb that agrees with the subject in simple sentences (using regular verbs).
   b. To select the correct form of a verb to agree with the subject in simple sentences, using "don't" or doesn't" (or other "problem" verbs).

Exercise 2
Evaluating Objectives Stated in Textbooks

Once we have some objectives for skills that the textbook teaches, it is a good idea to check to make sure that each objective contributes to the broad goals for our course and that no important objectives are omitted. For example, if our overall aim is the ability to use measuring devices in everyday life, we might want to revise the following objectives taken from the textbook exercises.

1. To state that there are three feet in a yard.
2. To state that both a yard and a foot ruler are used to measure "length" (as opposed to weight, temperature, hardness, and so forth).
3. To mark the yardstick and ruler in a group of pictures of measuring instruments when asked "Which measure length?"
4. To measure lines of different lengths to the nearest inch (all lines will be whole numbers of inches long from one to twelve).

Objective 1 is a knowledge objective. It is easily learned, but could be saved for a unit on converting feet to yards. Objectives 2 and 3 are concerned with the word "length" and with measuring devices. They are useful, but, like objective 1, are not critical for actual measuring. Objective 4 is directly related to the overall aim, but it does not go far enough. By visualizing what in his daily life a person might want to measure, we can see the need for a fifth objective: "to measure actual objects to the nearest inch on the foot ruler or foot on the yardstick."

Directions: Cross out the objectives below that do not contribute to the broad goal expressed in the "Introduction to the Series" and add one or two objectives you feel should be included on writing skills within the topic of "agreement between nouns and verbs."

Introduction to the Series: The *Charles English Series* presents a complete program in the development of writing skills, from simple narrative to more complicated assignments such as writing a poem, or article for publication.

Objectives for Unit on the Agreement of Subject and Verb:
1. To state that it is important for subject and verbs to agree in formal writing.
2. To select the form of a regular verb that agrees with the subject in simple sentences (and vice versa).
3. To circle the correct form of a verb used in a simple sentence, using forms that are commonly misused, such as "do" or "doesn't."
4.

5.

Answers
1. Number 1 should be crossed out. If you develop good writing skills, you do not need it, and if you fail to teach the student to have subject and verb agree, stating that it is important is of no use.
2 and 3. Selecting correct verb forms is not as relevant as original writing for the broad goal, but it is a first step in learning how to write. Unless the students are past this step, the objectives should be kept.

4. Because writing usually consists of producing rather than selecting, an objective requiring the student to write should be included. In addition, because the overall goal specifies various forms such as poem or article, it might be worthwhile to have an objective for each.

To refine our unit, we can check to see that none of Bloom's taxonomic categories is underrepresented. If few objectives fall in the higher categories (analysis, synthesis, or evaluation), we can try to think of more. Even a simple unit such as one on measuring with a ruler or yardstick can require skills that fall into these higher categories.

Some objectives for a unit of measuring are below. Note that they are all at Bloom's application level.

Bloom's Level	Objectives
Application	1. To measure lines and figures that are a whole number of inches or feet long (that is 3, not 3½ inches) and write down their length in inches or feet.
Application	2. To measure objects of various lengths and write their length to the nearest foot with a yardstick, or the nearest inch with a foot ruler.

If we stop and think, we can write some objectives that fall in other categories (see below), and in so doing make it more likely that the students' skills in measuring will transfer to daily life. Perhaps on a camping trip, with no rulers available, measurement is needed to set up a tent properly, or maybe in shop work a foreign part is given in metric units.

Comprehension	1. To identify the inches and feet in rulers of unfamiliar length (6-inches, 18-inches, 6-foot tape measure, and so forth).
Synthesis	1. To design his own measuring system, make his own ruler, name the units, and measure some objects with it.
Evaluation	1. To compare our measuring system with another one such as the metric system (or the students' products from synthesis

could be used), and describe at least two advantages each has over the other.

Directions: Improve the unit below by:
1. crossing out irrelevant objectives
2. writing the taxonomic level of each objective
3. adding objectives so that each of Bloom's categories is represented. (Refer as needed to previous chapters of this book.)

Overall Aim
To teach students how to read road maps to find information.

Bloom's Level: *Objectives Taken from the Exercises:*

_____   1. To state that a book of maps is called an atlas.
_____   2. To use a mileage key to find the distance between two cities shown as dots.
_____   3. To tell which towns you would pass through to get from one given city to another (using cities not used during instruction).
_____   4. To tell which of two cities is larger (using cities not used during instruction).

_____

_____

_____

_____

Answers
1. Objective 1 is irrelevant so far as reading road maps is concerned. It should be crossed out.
2. The categories in which the objectives fall are: (1) knowledge, (2) application, (3) comprehension (it is really a reading skill; application would be a possibility also, but what rule or method is being applied is open to question), and (4) comprehension (the student is translating symbols to answer questions).
3. No complete answer key can be given for your objectives, but some sample objectives for each category are given.

Analysis
To mark in different colors on a roadmap the interstate highway system, network of rivers and lakes, and state highway system, and tell how the three relate to each other. (Although a roadmap does not lend itself readily to analysis, there are different networks indicated on it that could be identified in an objective such as this one.)

Synthesis
To make an original roadmap that is easy to read and includes information a driver would want to know (hopefully some that current maps do not have).
To design a ten-hour sightseeing tour from a given town, to maximize interest and variety.

Evaluation
To tell which of two routes from point A to B would be better for speed, which for leisure, and which for economy, telling why.

Posttest

Directions: Either pick one of the sample minichapters on the following pages and write objectives for a unit using that material, or choose a section from a textbook you plan to use in teaching and use it to write objectives for a unit. You may find it helpful to refer to the Scoring Sheet on page 170 while writing the unit.

**PURPOSE OF SERIES SCIENCE YESTERDAY,
TODAY, AND TOMORROW**

The basic purpose of *Science Yesterday, Today, and Tomorrow* is to encourage scientific thinking and positive attitudes toward science. The series begins at the first grade with the development of an understanding of the scientific method and the acquisition of basic scientific skills and a relevant information base, and proceeds to build these abilities throughout the series. Some of the specific goals of the series are listed below:

1. To develop a better understanding of man and the way his body works.
2. To develop sound thinking habits through learning about the methods used in the sciences.
3. To gain an appreciation of the interdependence of living things and the importance of the natural world to man.
4. To provide experiences that will heighten the students' perception and appreciation of the natural and physical world around them.

The secret world of the ant can be a fascinating revelation to the 12-year-old. He is already familiar with ants, but may not know much about them. To stimulate interest, have students bring in ants and start an ant colony between two pieces of glass taped approximately ⅜ inch apart.

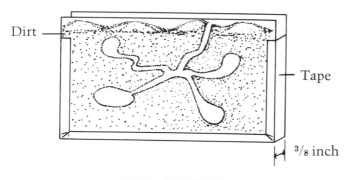

Dirt

Tape

⅜ inch

ANT COLONY

Point out the industriousness of the ants and their cooperation. Have students make careful observations about how the colony grows.

We have all seen ants. They can live almost anywhere. A crack in a sidewalk, a window box, or an old log—all make fine living quarters for ants.

An ant's eating habits are as varied as its living quarters. Drop a piece of ice cream on the sidewalk and soon it will be covered with ants. But though ants love sugar, their main food is dead insects. To this they add fruit and vegetable matter that is soft from rotting, or the sap from flowers or plants.

Ants are very strong. They can lift dead animals which weigh up to twenty times as much as they themselves. Imagine yourself lifting a dead cow! The ant transports its load by pushing and dragging it, constantly running around to check the best way to proceed.

Ants are social animals. They live in colonies, each ant helping the others with the basic work of raising children, storing food, building tunnels, and for the queen ants, laying eggs.

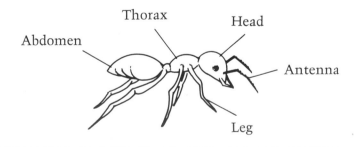

THE ANT

Because its body is divided into three sections—head, thorax, and abdomen—an ant is an insect.

Activity

Take a fresh apple and a rotten apple and place them both on a sidewalk. Later go out and see which one the ants are eating.

Can You Tell?
1. What does the ant eat?
2. Why does the author say that ants are social animals?
3. What are some other insects?

GENERAL AIMS

This textbook has been designed to extend the pupils' knowledge and appreciation of people in other times and places, and to develop positive attitudes toward the principles of freedom and peaceful coexistence. Specifically, it should help the pupil to reach the following understandings:

1. A single historical "fact" can be interpreted in many ways.
2. The freedom we have in the United States has been won through many bitter struggles.
3. Nations must cooperate to keep peace in the world.
4. The peoples of all nations are interdependent.

Teacher's Manual for Minichapter
on Zachary Taylor (eighth grade)

Purpose: To gain an understanding of the factors involved in the selection of a President through an analysis of Zachary Taylor's life.

Relating Concepts
1. Relate our war with Mexico to other wars such as the War of 1812 or the Civil War.
2. What was Mexico's viewpoint in the war?

AN EARNEST MAN

Zachary Taylor was born on November 24, 1784. He grew up on a plantation in Kentucky and at the age of twenty-four entered the army. Because of his bravery in defending a fort against an Indian attack during the War of 1812, he was promoted to captain.

Most of Taylor's young adult life was spent in military outposts, away from civilization, trying to maintain the army's hold on territories threatened by Indians. He recruited for the army, helped build roads, and created new frontier outposts.

The army had a series of successful encounters with the Seminole Indians in Florida's impenetrable swamps. In 1837, they sent Taylor to conquer the Seminoles. On Christmas day he attacked the Indians. Badly outnumbered, the Indians withdrew into the Everglades, but not before inflicting over 100 casualties on the army forces. Although the Indians were not beaten, the battle was hailed as a victory, and Taylor was promoted to brigadier general. He also got his nickname, "Old Rough and Ready," during this period.

Then, in 1846, there was trouble stirring on the Mexican border. Taylor was sent to "march to the Rio Grande." There he set up a fort just opposite the city of Metamoros. Though Fort Texas, as it was called, was well constructed, almost no provisions were made to protect its supply route north to Point Isabel. Taylor didn't seem to believe the Mexicans were really ready to fight, since the country had just had a revolution. He was in for a surprise. The Mexicans did attack. After a number of skirmishes they were driven back across the Rio Grande. Taylor did not pursue. His men were tired and he had not been foresighted enough to obtain material for pontoon bridges.

In spite of his tactical oversights, Taylor became commander of ever-increasing forces sent by Washington. The men were more than he could handle: Sickness broke out, and pillage, brawling, and general laxness ensued. Supplies did not keep pace with the men, and when Taylor was sent to take Monterrey, he had to leave several thousand men behind. With only about 7,000 men he attacked the well-fortified city, and, largely because of General Worth, finally overcame the city. As before, instead of following a victory with further attacks, Taylor rested. He was told to stay in Monterrey and learned that another general was being sent for an important battle in his stead. When unexpected reinforcements arrived, he advanced against orders. Then because he could not hold the city he captured, he returned to Monterrey and found only half of his men there. The rest had been taken by his rival, General Scott, who was moving on toward Mexico City. Taylor's thinly spread forces invited attack by the Mexicans. He advanced his headquarters a few miles and strengthened his defenses and his supply depot at Saltello.

The Mexican general, Santa Anna, who evidently didn't receive word about Scott's planned attack on Mexico City, made the long trek northward and attacked Taylor with 15,000 men. Taylor retreated toward Saltello with his 5,000 men. Thinking the Americans were in full flight, the Mexicans pursued. After their long march north across the desert with little water, little food, and no rest, the Mexicans ran into a solid American defensive position. The battle raged until dark. Tired, hungry, discouraged, the Mexicans retreated. Taylor had won largely because of Santa Anna's mistake.

Though his rival, General Scott, won the last battles in the war, the American people hailed "Old Rough and Ready" for "defeating" Santa Anna. In 1848, largely by default, Zachary Taylor became the twelfth President of the United States.

Questions

1. What kind of credentials and qualifications did Zachary Taylor have for the Presidency?
2. How does Zachary Taylor's rise to the Presidency compare with George Washington's?
3. Why does the author say that Taylor won the Presidency "by default"?

Report: Find an account of the war from the Mexican point of view. What did the Mexicans think of Zachary Taylor?

Scoring Sheet
You can evaluate your own unit as follows:

1. Check to see that you have at least one objective in each of Bloom's categories, and no more than 25 percent in the knowledge category.
2. Make sure all objectives are behavioral.
3. Make sure each objective relates to your overall goals for the subject matter, and that the skills described are useful for situations that can be encountered in everyday life.
4. As a final test to make sure that you have not dwelt on knowledge items, the following questions can be asked:
   a. Would an expert in the field be able to meet each objective as it is stated? (If not, your objective may depend on a particular phrasing to be memorized or on trivial details, and should be reevaluated.)
   b. Could a test item on the objective appear on an "open book" test? (When you permit students to use their textbooks and notes during a test, you are not likely to ask questions whose answers they can copy. The questions, therefore, are not likely to be at the knowledge level.)

If you have satisfied the first three criteria and can answer "Yes" to questions 4a and 4b, you have a good unit.

References

1. B. S. Bloom, M. D. Englehart, E. J. Furst, W. H. Hill, and D. R. Krathwohl, *A Taxonomy of Educational Objectives: Handbook I, the Cognitive Domain* (New York: McKay, 1956).
2. M. Wertheimer, *Productive Thinking* (New York: Harper & Row, 1959.)

Other Books on Behavioral Objectives

Gronlund, N. E. *Stating Behavioral Objectives for Classroom Instruction.* New York: Macmillan, 1970.

Kibler, R. J., L. L. Barker, and D. T. Miles. *Behavioral Objectives and Instruction.* Boston: Allyn & Bacon, 1970.

Lindvall, C. M. (ed.). *Defining Educational Objectives.* Pittsburgh: University of Pittsburgh Press, 1964.

Mager, R. F. *Preparing Instructional Objectives.* Palo Alto, Cal.: Fearon Publishers, 1962.

McAshan, H. H. *Writing Behavioral Objectives: A New Approach.* New York: Harper & Row, 1970.

Popham, W. J., and E. L. Baker. *Establishing Educational Goals.* Englewood Cliffs, N.J.: Prentice-Hall, 1970.

Index

73 74   7 6 5 4 3